Spiritual Awakening:

Look What Happened to Me. Is it Happening to You Too?

Spiritual Awakening

Look What Happened to Me.

Is it Happening to You Too?

JACQUELINE PARKER SCOTT, EdD, MBA

O and J Awakenings

2014

Copyright © 2014 by Jacqueline Parker Scott, EdD, MBA

All rights reserved. This book or any portion thereof may not be reproduced or used in any manner whatsoever without the express written permission of the publisher except for the use of brief quotations in a book review or scholarly journal.

First Printing: 2014

ISBN 978-0-9906644-0-6

Published By O and J Awakenings
PO Box 83632
Los Angeles, CA 90083

http://myspiritualawakenings.com

Dr. Jacqueline Parker Scott dedicates this book to:

The memory of my parents,
Thomas Aubrey Parker
and Daisy Singleton Parker

My children: Tres, Olympia, and Stephen, and grandchildren,
BreAzia, Logann, and Rachman, Jr.

My brothers and sisters: Harriet, Tonette, Thomas, Jr., Joseph, Gale,
April, and Renee

Contents

Preface	ix
Introduction	xiii
Chapter 1: Week 1: Jesus is Lord	1
Chapter 2: Week 2: God Our Father	19
Chapter 3: Week 3: Wholesome in Love	33
Chapter 4: Week 4: The Helper	43
Chapter 5: Week 5: Following Jesus	63
Chapter 6: Week 6: The Fruit of the Spirit	81
Chapter 7: Week 7: Spiritual Warfare	95
Chapter 8: Week 8: The Gifts of the Spirit	117
Chapter 9: Week 9: The Church Alive	137
Chapter 10: Conclusion	157
References/Spiritual Scriptures	161

Preface

When I began writing, Jesus gave me a message for this book, which I will reiterate below:

If you've opened this book, it means there is a message for you to receive. There are no mistakes in the universe. You are being divinely guided. It is up to you to continue your spiritual destiny. You have a free will. It is your decision to make.

This book is for the believer. It is for those who are beginning to receive their spiritual gifts, and for those who have already received their gifts and are aware of how others are receiving their gifts too. It is for those who are on or beginning their spiritual path. Everyone has a spiritual journey parallel to their earthly journey. You are either a minister in the pulpit or a minister among the people. Everyone has a spiritual assignment. You will receive your spiritual assignment at various times and ages. Some people receive them as children. Some people do not receive them until later in life. You already have your spiritual gifts, but you will develop them when you are ready. You have a free will to decide to develop your sixth sense, so to speak. It is up to you.

This book gives you an idea of how Spiritual gift(s) works. Everyone has their own testimony of spiritual experiences. You have a choice. You will choose good or evil. You will not get to heaven without going through Me, Jesus Christ. I am the life and the truth. Those who are interested in developing their spirituality will continue reading. Those who are not ready yet will put the book down for later. Everyone who receives this book is meant to read it.

I was divinely guided to write my spiritual and supernatural experiences and to share them with you. If you are reading this message and you do not recall any supernatural experiences of your own, this book will prepare you as you experience them.

This is no extraordinary book. It is an example of my experiences of charismatic faith. Some people will be able to relate to my experiences with their own. Others will understand once they begin their very special relationship with Jesus Christ. Many will speak to the Holy Spirit. The chosen few will speak directly to Jesus Christ. Know the Trinity—God the Father, the Son, and the Holy Spirit are one. When you speak to the Holy Spirit, you are also speaking to Jesus Christ and to God.

I am keeping it real. I'm constantly wondering if the things that have happened to me have also happened to you. How many of us have tried to rationalize our supernatural experiences? How many mentally ill people are possessed with evil and trapped in their own bodies? Who is investigating the supernatural experiences people are having?

I am telling my story—a part of my life—my supernatural and my spiritual life with Jesus Christ. I am baptized in the Spirit. I have a very special relationship with Jesus. I accept Him into my heart. He leads me and guides me step by step. I do not worry. I know that Jesus loves me, takes care of me, protects me, provides for me, and He is with me 24/7.

Jesus Christ told me to write this book about my experiences when I took a nine-week seminar in September 2009. Jesus told me the title of this book in 2007, two years before I took the seminar. I was told in 2011 to write my book. In 2014, Jesus told me it is time to publish.

Introduction

In the beginning of your spiritual quest, you might wonder if it is real. You might ask yourself, "Is this really happening to me?" Or you might wonder if it is happening to someone else. You might feel crazy at times, but supernatural experiences that occur on a spiritual quest cannot be proven scientifically. Working with a spiritual partner will help you feel like you are in touch with reality even though the supernatural activities continue to take place. The purpose of this book is to talk about my spiritual awakening I experienced at a nine-week seminar I attended in September through November of 2009 at my church through a charismatic prayer group.

My spiritual journey first started when I went to a healing mass service at my church in October of 2004. I wanted my oldest daughter to go, because I was concerned for her well-being and hoped the healing mass would help her. When I told her about it, she agreed to meet me there.

So, I went to the healing mass on Friday, October 29, 2004. I had never been to a healing mass before. A visiting priest presided over the healing mass service. I always went to church (mass) on Sunday morning, so I was unaccustomed to being at a mass service on a Friday evening. I told myself, "Wow, it's so nice to be here this evening."

During the mass, the priest instructed us to hum while he prayed in tongues. He sectioned us off. I was glad I was sitting on the side near the alto section and not the sopranos. I cannot harmonize so I will try and sing in the tone of whom ever is standing next to me. I am a true alto. What an experience. I cannot express the feeling that flushed through my body. Little did I know what was in store for me that night.

After mass, the priest told us that he did not heal. He was a vessel for the Lord. The Lord heals. This is no hoax. If you see someone fallout from the Holy Ghost, do not fall out because they did. The difference is that when you fall out from the Holy Spirit, you will not hurt yourself. The priest went on to say, "If you fall out on your own, we may have to call the paramedics, and you may have to go to the hospital. If you get hurt falling, you did not have the Holy Ghost experience."

Then the priest walked down the aisle, pointed his finger, and said, "Someone in this section has a burning sensation in their stomach." A man started to stand, but the priest interrupted and said, "Do you have a burning sensation in your stomach?"

The man said, "Not exactly."

The priest said, "No, it is not you." He repeated, "Someone in this section has a burning sensation in their stomach." Another man stood up, and the priest said, "Go to the altar." He turned to the left and said, "On this side, someone has trouble with their knees. Go to the altar." He turned to his right and said, "Someone over here has migraine headaches. Go to the altar."

Then it happened . . . the priest turned and pointed in my direction, and said, "Over here, a mother is worried about her older daughter who does not live with her. She is going to be all right. Come up to the altar." The priest's head was down when he pointed directly at me. When he lifted his head, it was as if someone was lifting me up, sort of nudging me to stand. So, I got up, and the priest said, "Go to the altar," and so I went.

As I walked to the altar, I was in disbelief that the priest had known that I was worried about my oldest daughter. I knelt at the altar with the others that he called up and waited for his anointing. Before he anointed the congregation, he anointed us individually at the altar one by one.

Finally, it was my turn. He stood in front of me. I was kneeling, with my head bowed, and my hands clasped in the prayer position. He held my hands, and I told him that I was worried about my oldest daughter. He prayed with me and told me again that she was going to be all right.

At that moment, my body relaxed like spaghetti. I screamed and fell backward in a kneeling position. I was lying on my back, and as I lay there, crying and praying, I told God that I completely surrendered to Him. I also prayed for my younger daughter, protection for her daughter, my son, my sister, and my brother-in-law's mother, who was very ill.

When I fell backward, everything went black, and although my eyes were closed, I saw a black Bible. I cried and prayed. Finally, I opened my eyes. People were walking by, kneeling over me, touching my hands, and praying. Two men were smiling at me. One of them in particular looked like an angel. His smile was so pure and filled with such love. His eyes were bright with a glow in them. He seemed so peaceful. I felt safe and calm from his presence.

The two men helped me up, and I went back to the altar. Everything happened so fast. I wanted the priest to pray with me for my other children. The priest came over to me. After he prayed with me, I stayed at the altar and continued praying. The priest came back to pray with me again. This time he put both hands on my head and bent over to whisper in my ear. He said, "You can bless your own children because we are all vessels for the Lord. They only have to believe in Jesus Christ before they can be blessed, but you can bless them." We prayed again. After that, I was able to leave the altar.

I walked down the middle of the aisle with my head down and my eyes staring at the floor. When I reached the back of the church, I turned around, blessed myself with holy water, made the sign of the cross, and left the church.

It was such a wonderful feeling. I was completely relaxed. I had never been blessed and touched by the Holy Spirit before. I called my younger daughter when I got into the car. I also called my sister to tell her about the experience.

I remember totally surrendering to Jesus our Lord God. What is still unbelievable to me was the way I fell backward. It was such an awkward position. I fell on my back, but my legs were still in the kneeling position. I wasn't sore at all. I felt physically and mentally great. I had never experienced that kind of feeling in my entire life. Since then, I've tried to lie in that position, but I can't do it.

This happened in 2004, but I can still feel the wonderful experience of that moment. Oh, God is good, all the time. All the time, God is good. Alleluia.

Sometime before the healing mass service, I started reading the book, *The Purpose Driven Life*, by Rick Warren. I didn't read it straight through. I read this book off and on from September 2004 until February 2005. After reading it, I knew I was a minister among the people as one of the people. When people came to me for help, I knew that Jesus was answering their prayers. I don't know why I would say, "I am helping you because of God who is answering your prayer for help through me. This would just be a thought that came into my mind. Little did I know what was in store for me.

I continued to help people who were praying to Jesus. I helped several of my colleagues with their dissertations and I talked to others who came to me who discussed their concerns in life. I continued helping in this way until I received my first encounter to deliver a message from Jesus to someone who was not expecting it. It was awesome.

On August 5, 2007, Jesus told me to give a message to a minister. Over several weeks, the minister had been on my mind. Thoughts would come about him as if it was a message to give to him, but I didn't write them down, and it didn't make that much sense to me at the time. Well, early that Sunday morning, at 12:53 a.m., I had my third thought about the minister. I can't quite explain the feeling, but after those three thoughts that kept coming to my mind—"Stay the course. Don't waver. Only you know what God wants for you"—I decided to write them down.

As I began to write, I would have a thought and then I would write it. I would then have another thought and would write it down before another thought would come. I did not paraphrase—I wrote this message for the minister that came from God exactly the way the thoughts came to me. God said,

Stay the course, do not waver, only you know what God wants to tell you. One day, you will be on TV preaching the word, not nationwide, but worldwide. God has put a special anointing on you, and He has special things for you to do. You know what He has for you. God has given you special talents to administer the word to the people. Do not waver. Stay the course. You are the chosen one. You have special gifts from God. Stay the course. Do not waver. God has a lot in store for you. Stay the course. Do not waver. Do not give up. God has a plan for you. You will know because God will let you know. He has plans for you. This is a special message from God. You have prayed for the answer. This is the answer to your prayer.

I thanked God for allowing me to be the vessel, the instrument to give the minister his message. I was ever so humble and honored to give the minister such a special message from God.

I then prayed to God to let me know when was I to give the minister the message. Then a thought rushed through my mind—the minister goes to church at 7:00 a.m.

As I sat for a few minutes, thoughts continued to come, but this second message was for me. *"My prophecy abilities are to give messages to people who have prayed for answers. I will relay the answers from God to the people who have prayed for them. I give them in different ways. I can give the answer by telling them or by helping them."*

I went to sleep and woke up just before 7:00 a.m. I called and left a message for the minister to call me before going to church. I was a little nervous at first, because this was the first strong message of stay the course from God that I was to relay. I had been working for years helping people. When people came to me for help, I already knew they had prayed for help. This was the first time I told God's message and I knew it would not be the last. I was happy that the minister accepted the message of stay the course and knew it was true by what the message meant to him. He asked me to e-mail the message to him and I did.

I told him that the message kept repeating stay the course. I thought it was redundant but the minister said he needed to hear it that many times. While the message didn't mean much to me, the minister receiving the message knew exactly what it meant.

A few days later on August 7, 2007, at ten in the morning, I was sitting under the dryer at the beauty shop and a message came to me from God.

When you are invited to give a speech, you will be delivering a message, so take this one step further and answer prayers for God through:

1 *Helping people;*
2 *Giving exact messages to a particular person at a particular time;*
3 *Answering prayers in a speech;*

You are to pray before you deliver any answers for God in any way that you may answer them. When you give or deliver a message, only that person will know that their prayers have been answered.

You are to write a book about your spiritual experiences. You will name the book, Spiritual Awakening: Look What Happened to Me. Is it Happening to You Too?

Right after this revelation, I got a little nervous. This was new to me, and the messages were coming faster than usual. It was like the messages could come at any time and any place.

I continued to work for Jesus as September 2009 approached, when I attended the church prayer-group seminar. I became curious how one communicated with Jesus. I would hear people say all the time, "Jesus told me," or "The Holy Spirit told me," and I wondered how they heard it. I was thinking of someone talking in your ear with sound rather than thought. I wanted to become closer to Jesus and I thought attending the prayer-group seminar would help me with that connection . . . and it did.

Until that point, I knew Jesus told me that I would prophesy and give messages to people. I wanted a more intimate relationship with Jesus, but I didn't know how to get it. The seminar helped me have that special relationship with Jesus Christ on a more consistent basis where I would learn how to communicate with Him every day. This was a nine-week seminar. We were given scriptures and "food for thought" to read every day. I had a wonderful experience in receiving my charismatic gifts. I would like to walk you through my nine-week charismatic renewal of faith in the parish seminar sponsored by the parish weekly prayer group. Let's take one week at a time of my relationship I developed with our Lord, Jesus Christ.

Chapter 1

Week 1: Jesus Is Lord

"Jesus explained to them: 'I am the bread of life; whoever comes to me will never hunger, and whoever believes in me will never thirst'" (John 6:35, 37)

The seminar started on Friday September 25, 2009, from 7:00 to 9:00 p.m. It was a cozy setting; the room felt more like a den in a home than a classroom setting. The cozy, comfortable sofa-like chairs were set up in a circle. Our group leaders were a married couple who shared in the leadership role for the seminar. There were around thirty-five participants who introduced ourselves, and then we were put into smaller groups to discuss our spiritual experiences. I was fascinated with the different experiences we all shared that night.

We were given food for thought to carry us through the week. The main theme for week one was "Jesus is Lord." We met on Friday evenings and started our week of meditation and prayer on Saturday. I took this seminar seriously. I was so excited about the seminar that I forgot to write about my experiences on the first Friday seminar meeting. I started documenting my experiences on Saturday the very next day remembering everything I could for the first week seminar meeting.

In week one, I felt the love for Jesus. I realized for the first time that I could communicate with Him. I could always talk to Him and pray the Lord's Prayer (Matt. 6:9–13); but now I can have a two-way conversation with Him in prayer. We have to learn how to be still and listen to His Word. There are many ways to pray, such as praise and worship (Ps. 66:1–4), forgiveness (Eph. 1:15–16), thanksgiving (Eph. 6:18), intercession (Thess. 5:17), petition (Phil. 4:6-7), tongues (1 Cor. 14:2, 15) and listening (1 Kings 19:8–15). The hardest part is listening to the Holy Spirit talk to you. Just be still and ask the Holy Spirit to speak to you. Wait, be quiet, and write down the thoughts that come to your mind. At first, you may only hear or think of one word that comes to your mind. In time, you will receive a phrase, then a paragraph, and maybe even pages.

Listening to the Holy Spirit takes time to train yourself to hear Him. You have to focus on listening without distraction from the things around you. Listening to the Holy Spirit is like learning how to ride a bike. You will first have to learn how to balance yourself. It may take a while. Then you will learn how to balance and ride at the same time. You will balance and ride for short stretches and then all of a sudden you will take off riding the bike for longer distances. The same thing happens when you learn how to listen to the Holy Spirit in prayer.

I am an associate professor at a community college where I teach computer classes. I remember one of my students from school who was learning how to listen to the Holy Spirit and was having a hard time listening during prayer. At first, she would not hear anything nor would any thoughts come to her mind. For several days nothing would happen. And then it finally came, one word. The Holy Spirit said, "Focus." I remember when she came to me and said, "Focus."

I said, "What?"

She said, "Focus. That is what the Holy Spirit told me today."

We rejoiced together. She had the big breakthrough. She then went on to more words, then paragraphs, and possibly even pages.

If you have not been able to reach the Holy Spirit yet in your life, the time is now. After praying to the Lord as you usually do, ask the Holy Spirit to speak to you. Wait patiently and listen. Have a journal ready so you can write down what you hear or the thoughts that come to your mind. After you finish writing it, you will go back and read what the Holy Spirit told you for the day.

In the seminar, we were given the book, *Thy Kingdom Come*, written by Dominic Berardino, which helped us to connect to the Holy Spirit with daily readings. The book contained scriptures and small readings that inspired us each day as we learned to become closer to Jesus. The seminar helped me to connect and pray to Jesus every day. Going through the daily readings were very rewarding.

It is wonderful to know you can talk to the Holy Spirit yourself and get a response. I enjoyed the different topics that the book took us through to understand how to connect with Jesus. Each person may receive a different message according to his or her own individual experiences.

In week one, I learned to understand that I have a relationship with Jesus, that He talks to me, and I can talk to Him. I realized that I would have a stronger responsibility than people coming to me for help, and that they came to me because Jesus was answering their prayers. For example, they would pray for assistance with completing their dissertations in their doctoral program.

In the first week of this nine-week seminar, I was asking Jesus questions and He was answering me. He taught me how to be still and quiet so I could listen to Him.

The next seven days in week one are my actual journal entries during the 2009 seminar.

Week 1, Day 1: Saturday, September 26, 2009

Today I get it. I now understand that Mother Teresa of Calcutta got it—pure love. We must love, respect, be gentle, and be kind to people as if we are talking to Jesus our Lord, our Savior. This earthly world is materialistic with evil thoughts and connotations. We are here for spiritual development. We can obtain spiritual development with or without earthly riches. We will not be able to sustain ourselves without

Jesus. We are our thoughts. We create our own world, but you cannot do it alone. You must have Jesus.

"Jesus explained to them: 'I am the bread of life; whoever comes to me will never hunger, and whoever believes in me will never thirst. Everything the Father gives me will come to me, and I will not reject anyone who comes to me" (John 6:35, 37).

Know that Jesus will never turn away from us. Our earthly experiences are for reasons. As we move away from Jesus, things happen in our lives and we make choices with our free will. As we move away from Jesus, circumstances come into our lives to learn lessons for our spiritual development. If we don't get it (spiritual development lesson) things will get worse. You can become an alcoholic, anorectic, compulsive over-eater, workaholic, etc. When you go to Jesus, He will never let you down. He will lift you up and put you back on track to your Divine purpose in life.

For the universe, earth is like an electronic game. Spiritual beings come down to play the game of earth. The question is, "Do you know the rules of the 'earth' game"? The earth game has various rules, and there are many choices to make. That's why we have free will to be able to make these choices. We all know right from wrong. We choose our lifestyle and living conditions. It is from within you that causes the problems, not from the outside world. It is not until we understand that it is you from within, and not them from outside, that is causing your world to be what it is.

The rules are really simple for me:

1. Know that you are the captain of your own ship, not someone else.

2. It is never too late to turn your life around, but know that you cannot do it alone; you will need Jesus our Lord God, our Savior.

3. Know that you are never alone in this earthly place; you always have Jesus Christ.

4. Never feel hate. Hate destroys the spirit; it is like throwing darts at it. Every time you hate on someone you are hurting yourself.

5. Life is one big balloon, and one dart can pop it. So, be careful in what you say and do. We are all a part of the universe—this one big balloon. Be gentle, kind, loving, and respectful to everyone you see and meet. Even those on the streets who beg to survive are God's children just trying to make it in this earthly place, this game of life on earth.

6. You know right from wrong, and you make your own choices. Accept the consequences of your actions and don't place the blame on someone else.

7. When in need, lean on Jesus Christ for help. Prayers work. Be specific in your prayers. "It is better to be lead from He who is in you than he who is in the world" (1 John 4:4).

Week 1, Day 2: Sunday, September 27, 2009

"You are well acquainted with the favor shown you by our Lord Jesus Christ: how for your sake he made himself poor though he was rich, so that you might become rich by his poverty" (2 Cor. 8:9).

Jesus came down from heaven to share His wealth of the Kingdom of Heaven with us who are poor in spirit. All of the money in the world doesn't mean anything without a rich spirit. Look at the many people who commit suicide, fall prey to drugs, or many other vices because they do not have faith in Jesus Christ. We are here to strengthen our spirit and to develop our soul. For you see, God is good. Jesus Christ is our Lord and Savior. Many times we think we may know it all, but we can only learn a minuscule of the knowledge of the universe. There is so much to understand in the human race. It all boils down to one word—love. Your health depends on love. Life depends on love.

As we go along in life, we must understand who we are, why we are here, and live a Christian life. No one will get into heaven without being a Christian. You will have to come back to earth to start all over again until you get it right.

As I was praying and meditating, Jesus said to me:

You are here to learn about Jesus and to live a Christian life. You are here taking this seminar because you seek to have a better understanding and a better relationship with Jesus in your heart. Seek and you shall find. Ask and you shall be answered. Go now in peace and wait for day three.

Oh Jesus, thank you, thank you, thank you. I am learning how to reach out to you. To be quiet and listen to what you have to say. I am learning we can talk, communicate, and have a two-way conversation.

These are some thoughts that came to me throughout day two.

1. People have mentioned to me that I am like a Mother Teresa. They also said I was a prophetess and that I was very spiritual. All I really want to do is to be obedient to Jesus. Don't get caught up on Christian religion. For example, don't get caught up on types of cars. Each car has the same function to get you where you want/need to go. It's the same for Christian religion. It's the Christian religion that gets you to your spiritual destination (heaven) through Jesus Christ. I believe in God, Jesus Christ, and the Holy Spirit.

2. Discernment: Someone said to me, I knew it wasn't God who told me because it told me to do something that I knew was wrong. Jesus will never tell you to do something wrong, bad, or evil.

3. I am uncluttering my house as I unclutter my mind.

I received a message from God for one of my students at school. I am an associate professor at a community college. I have a master's in business administration (MBA) and a doctorate in education (EdD).

I was working on my schoolwork on a Sunday morning around 11:30 when a name of a student started coming to me. I could see him. I knew that God wanted me to deliver a message to this student. This happened once before when I had a message to deliver to a minister. The interesting thing is that the person is unaware that I am bringing a message from God. I am only the messenger. I wrote the message exactly the way it was given to me in thoughts.

At the time, I was busy with my schoolwork, and at first I didn't want to stop. However, I quickly stopped, relaxed, and asked Jesus if He wanted me to stop what I was doing to take the message. He said, "Yes." I don't know what I was thinking questioning the Lord. I guess it was just my human nature kicking in at the time. I quickly corrected myself and became obedient.

This student is a Veteran who recently returned to the United States from Iraq and was having a hard time adjusting to civilian life.

Here is the message for my student from Jesus Christ.

Sunday, September 27, 2009, 11:30 a.m.

I know it is hard for you to readjust into mainstream society. It is harder than the people around you will ever know. They have no clue what you have been through. I know it is not easy, but you can overcome and be able to help other people like yourself. God has special plans for you. You are to work hard at getting yourself together. You are going a little slower than planned. Listen, you can overcome this, and you will. It is up to you to decide how long it's going to take you. This is what you need to do: start believing in God again. Know that you are not alone. Many soldiers that have returned went through the same thing you are going through. You are not alone; you have Jesus. You cannot do it without Him. Start praying every day before you start your day. I will lead you, your God, your savior. Remember, God is blessing you every day, but you have to do your part. Now go, be obedient, and pray every day.

Thank you, Jesus.

Week 1, Day 3: Monday, September 28, 2009

It was said in the day-three reading that "Jesus Christ is worthy of our allegiance to him" (Berardino, 8).

"Our attitude must be that of Christ . . ." (Phil. 5:5–11).

It is difficult to change our old habits. Yet, to enter into the Kingdom of Heaven, many of us will need to do so. Partnering with a spiritual person will help this process. Sometimes working with someone will help you to stay the course. We can do it. It takes effort on our part.

Jesus said to me:

I want to help you, but you have to help yourself. Everyone wants someone else to do it for them. That is not how it works. You have to take responsibility for yourself. It is not an easy task, but it can be done. Go in peace. Stay peaceful. Do not get yourself upset. Love, peace, and happiness will heal you. You have the stamina to do what is right even when it may not appear to be the right thing to do. God is watching over you. You are learning how to have the relationship with God that you've always wanted. You can speak to God every day, and God will speak to you every day. Do not question God. Be obedient.

Jesus, am I on the right path? Am I doing what I am supposed to be doing?

Yes.

But I'm not quite sure what I'm supposed to be doing. I feel there is something that you want me to do, but I don't know what it is.

You will know when the time comes. Just be obedient.

I know the difference of your voice from others. I now can understand when you have a message for someone. I wavered with the student Veteran's message. I even asked if you wanted me to stop working. I am sorry for that. I am learning. I should know if you stop me from work to do something else that you will let me have enough time to do what I need to do because you will fulfill all of my needs. Thank you, Lord, for being here for me.

It's time. Wait for day four.

Thank you, Jesus.

***

Here are some thoughts that came to me throughout day three.

For some reason, after saving my notes and the message from Sunday, I read one of my files pertaining to my response after my first message from God to deliver to a minster prior to his Sunday sermon on August 5, 2007. I know I was meant to read this journal entry today that was written a day after I delivered the message.

Monday, August 6, 2007—Journal Entry

After delivering my first message from God to the minister, I am really beginning to realize the real power of prayer. We often talk about it but never really digest the true meaning of it. There are so many signs with answers all around us, but sometimes we are not paying attention to the little things that happen in our lives.

After reading this journal entry, I remember being at a mothers' convention in Houston in July when I was asked by a mother also attending the conference how I felt about being the mother of my children. I gave the earthly answers. "Oh, I am proud of them. We are a family," etc. It was mentioned to me by the mother that God had chosen me to birth my children just like He chose Mary to birth Jesus. Now she really caught my attention, because at first, I was just doing what I call "small talk". She went on to say, "God has chosen you." At the time, I told her I knew what she said was from God and that there are no mistakes in the universe. I was meant to hear this today, and I thanked her for delivering the message to me. We praised God together. I knew I was chosen to birth my children, and I am proud of all of them. I have two daughters and a son.

It was like God was bringing me back to my spiritual center. You know that sometimes we can stray away. I know now I was chosen to deliver my first message to the minister on August 5, 2007. I knew exactly what the message said. I went and sought the minister to deliver the message at a specific time, the minister who was in deep prayer waiting for God's answer.

For a long time, I have been a vessel, an instrument for God, but I am moving to another level. I didn't ask for this—it has been assigned to me by God—and I so humbly accept my assignment. It was like I needed to re-affirm my commitment to God's assignment to me. Yes, Lord, I so humbly accept my assignment. I thank you for choosing me. I will be obedient.

Week 1, Day 4: Tuesday, September 29, 2009

I don't know why, but I know that I am hurting inside, dear Jesus. The thought that we were sinners and you still died for us . . .

". . . It is precisely in this that God proves his love for us: that while we were still sinners, Christ died for us" (Rom. 5:6–8).

In prayer I thought: I don't want to get too emotional and block my communication with you. I enjoy our quiet time together each day. I like when you communicate with me. Please don't stop. I need your love in my life too. I want you to continue to care about us on earth. I know I will not get to heaven without you. Is there anything Lord that you want to say to me?

You are a good person, a tender, loving caring person. You have love for many people. You don't know how many people love and care about you. Don't give up. Keep going. Everything is going to work itself out. Just have patience. You are on a mission. The ball is in place, and it is rolling now and can't be stopped. You will be happy again. The time is very near. Hold on and continue the path that you are on. Wait for day five.

Thank you, Jesus, for your presence. I do love you and I do feel better. I love you very much. I am so lucky to be graced with your presence.

Week 1, Day 5: Wednesday, September 30, 2009

In day five, it was mentioned that "Man-made religions and philosophies are people's attempts to reach God, whereas Christianity is God reaching man through Jesus Christ" (Berardino, 9).

I believe that Jesus Christ came down from heaven to save our souls. Thank you, Jesus, for your sacrifice to allow us to stay on track to the Kingdom of Heaven. I love you, Jesus, and I want to get closer to you. I want to live a good life and be a good soldier for you and our God. I want to live a peaceful life helping others to learn how to live a Christian peaceful life. I believe that it is done unto you as you believe. I believe in Jesus Christ.

Oh, Jesus, please help me be a good person and a good Christian. I do love you. Thank you for giving me this opportunity to serve you. I gave your message to my student. He was so relieved and receptive to receiving it. Thank you for using me as a vessel for your message. I am honored and so appreciative in serving you. Oh, dear Jesus, good morning. I am here waiting to continue to serve you. I do want a closer relationship with you. I do want to continue to serve you. I walk in the white light of Jesus Christ.

When I help people, I know that they have been praying for help. I often tell people when I help them, "It is not I but Jesus Christ, the Father above." Some would even cry because they knew it was the truth. They had been praying. I feel good helping Christians find their way, their spiritual path. I am finding my way, my spiritual path. I know that I am a minister among the people as one of the people, not as a minister on the pulpit in the church. Oh, dear Jesus, guide me, lead me, and show me the way.

"Jesus told him, "I am the way, and the truth and the life; no one comes to the Father but through me" (John 14:6).

Dear Jesus, do you have something to tell me today?

Yes, I do. You are to lead people, help people learn about me. Be patient, wait on the Lord. Go slow. We are not in a hurry. This is an eternal life we are developing. You have gifts, spiritual gifts that are, in time, for you to use. You have used some of them, but there are more to develop now. Go in peace and wait for day six.

Thank you, Jesus.

Week 1, Day 6: Thursday, October 1, 2009

"Jesus Christ leads us into the glory of God the Father . . ." (Berardino, 9).

I know Jesus is leading me and He has been leading me for a while. It is one of the reasons I am taking this seminar. I want to understand and get closer to Jesus. I know that I am a vessel for Jesus to use to help other spirits that are here. I so graciously accept. I am beginning to understand that I am lead by Jesus. I will be obedient to Him.

Jesus, is there anything you want to say this morning?

Yes. You are doing just fine. Everything is going according to plan. Keep doing what you are doing. Everything is going to work out. You are doing the Lord's work. You have been doing it for some time now. You now know how to tap into the universe. Go now and wait for day seven.

Thank you, Jesus.

Week 1, Day 7: Friday, October 2, 2009

". . . Jesus Christ is supreme in every way over all creation and also over the new creation—His Body, the church . . ." (Berardino, 10).

"He is the image of the visible God, the firstborn of all creatures. In him everything in heaven and on earth was created, things visible and invisible, whether thrones of dominions principalities or powers; all were created through Him, and for Him . . . It is He who is the head of the body, the church; He who is the beginning, the first born of the dead, so that primacy may be His in everything . . . " (Col. 1:15–20).

This morning I feel that I just need to be still, and listen to what Jesus has to say.

Good morning, dear Jesus. This morning I am here to listen to what you have to say.

Be still and listen, my child. You are the chosen one. You have lots of God's work to do. Sometimes it will not be easy, but you will be able to accomplish it. Many people need God's help. God will use you to help them. You will know when the time comes. You are beginning to know when I am speaking directly to you. You can discern. This is a gift— not everyone has this gift, but you have it so use it wisely. The beginning and the end, Omega . . . you will know what that means later.

For now, continue learning how to become closer to God, to me. You will understand later what my plans are for you. You must keep the faith and continue on your path. Go now in peace.

Thank you, Jesus.

***

As the week ended, I looked back to see what I had learned. I took this seminar to have a better relationship with Jesus. It was exciting to know how I was able to reach out to Him. I learned how to be quiet and listen to what He had to say. I had a two-way conversation with Him. He even gave me an assignment to deliver a message to a student Veteran at school where I teach. I learned how to listen with patience to take one step at a time. I know I am a vessel, an instrument for God. Jesus let me know that we are not in a hurry, for this is an eternal life we are developing. I know God will use me to help His people.

Chapter 2

Week 2: God Our Father

"There is one Lord, one faith, one baptism, one God, and Father of all, who is over all, and works through all, and is in all" (Ephesians 4:5, 6)

On Friday evening of October 2, 2009, we broke into groups to share spiritual information. On this night, we shared what God meant to us, which referred to the second week's Topic, "God Our Father." After our sharing, the group leader came up to me and told me I had the gift of prophecy and God confirmed this by telling us things in threes (I have now been told I have the gift of prophecy twice). She asked me if I could speak in tongues. I told her no. She believed a prophet could speak in tongues. She told me to ask Jesus about being able to speak in tongues because there was a spiritual warfare and the devil would try to attack you.

At that moment, I recalled when I was in northern California at a conference several years ago. When a group of us from the conference were in a hotel in the hospitality suite, a woman I had just met at the conference came up to me and whispered in my ear, "The devil comes up to you and stops right in front of you."

I said to her, "I know because I walk in the white light of Jesus Christ." The woman walked away and I never encountered her again. In remembering this, I wasn't concerned at all what the group leader said about the devil could attack me.

When we broke into groups, I talked about the messages Jesus told me to give to the minister and to a student who had recently returned from Iraq. I also talked about the experiences with my oldest daughter when she was young; she used to have dreams and visions that she knew would come true.

I remember the morning when my older daughter was around eight years old and she came down the stairs crying about a dream she had about her pet rabbit. She said she saw the rabbit dead in its cage, and a cloth was covering the top of the cage. When she told me what happened, I told her not to worry because it was just a dream. She told me it was one of her dreams she knew would come true. I wondered what she was talking about. Well, a few weeks later, her dream came true. The rabbit died just like she said with the cloth over the cage.

I knew then that she had special gifts, which led to my curiosity about paranormal phenomena. At that time, I watched TV shows like *One Step Beyond*. I really didn't connect my oldest daughter's special gifts with the Holy Spirit or Jesus. I actually looked at my oldest daughter's "special gifts" as being psychic. I just didn't know any better then. My oldest daughter learned not to talk about it a lot.

Another woman in the seminar talked about when she gets mad at a person. She would say to herself that something bad would happen to the person, and it would happen. Everyone was silent. We didn't say a word. It was as if I could see a sense of evil in her eyes. I remember her coming up to me quietly after the group session was over. It felt like a snake was coming up behind me. She asked me if I was coming back next week. I told her yes. She smiled and walked away as if she had sneaked in to talk to me. I didn't understand why she felt she needed to sneak around or if it was just how she made me feel.

That night, I turned off the nightstand lamp in my room. As I lay down to go to sleep, something grabbed me, held me, and wouldn't let me go. I felt a pillow on my face. At first, I struggled to set myself free, but then I began to rebuke it in the name of Jesus Christ, and it released me right away. I say "it" because I really don't know what "it" was. This was not the first time that something of this nature had happened to me. I do know that I do not fear "it," for Jesus Christ is at my side. The devil feeds off fear. I do not fear the devil, for Jesus is more powerful than the devil will ever be. Good overpowers evil. Have faith and faith will set you free.

During week two, I realized that I was a soldier of God. What an exciting feeling. I would protect others. It was in my destiny to protect others. Jesus told me that He would show me how I would do it. Little did I know that I would be casting out demons. He told me that I was a child of God. No harm would come to me. Evil would be afraid of me.

Jesus told me that I was the chosen one and to not let other people get in my way of my divine path. He told me that I did not have to impress anyone and to just be my own person. People who I needed would come in contact with me naturally. He told me to continue to read the Bible. I really didn't read the Bible much until I started having this special relationship with Jesus.

During week two, I realized that miracles were happening around us all the time, but sometimes we don't realize it or recognize them even when we specifically ask for them.

Here are my journal entries for week two.

Week 2, Day 1: Saturday, October 3, 2009

"Everyone has been given over to me by my Father. No one knows the Son but the Father, and no one knows the Father but the son—and anyone to whom the son wishes to reveal him" (Matt. 11:27).

Just like there is a bond of love between Jesus and God, I want to have the same bond of love with Jesus and God. I feel this seminar is helping me to bond with Jesus and God. I have questions for Jesus from last night's seminar meeting. The group leader spoke about speaking in tongues. I have heard people speaking in tongues. I actually heard the person who leads us in songs speak in tongues. The group leader said we needed to ask about speaking in tongues.

Dear Jesus, what are speaking in tongues, and do I need to speak it?

You will eventually speak in tongues but not now. When the time comes, you will speak in tongues. For now, focus on learning more about me, Jesus Christ, your Lord, your Savior. You will have many gifts from God. You have been chosen for a purpose. You will know when the time comes. Be patient, my dear child, be patient. Everything prospers at the right time. Have faith in me and no one else. I will direct you. I know you are faithful. There are a few things to develop at this time before you receive the gift of tongues. Be patient. Your time will come. Continue down your path, your divine path. Go now and wait for day two.

Thank you, Jesus.

***

Here are the thoughts I had throughout day one of the second week.

Jesus came to me and said:

You will speak in the groups with a message for each person. They will know what the message says. You just need to deliver it. You will talk about your experiences with them, which will open them up to talk about theirs. Each week you will encounter someone new to the group. Eventually, you will know each person in the groups. They are fascinated with your experiences and are going to want to know more. You are only to speak with them about your experiences in the groups and seminar, not outside of the seminar. Some of the people at the seminar are not spiritually based. They are earth-bound with evil, so beware, but do not be afraid, for I am with you. Do not fear and do not back down. You carry the Word of the Father. Go in peace.

Thank you, Jesus.

I called my spiritual partner, my sister. I told her what the Lord told me about speaking in tongues. Little did I know that she spoke in tongues. She had to refresh my memory. When we went to a healing mass, I remembered that she had spoken in tongues. She asked Jesus for the gift. And then all of a sudden, while we were talking, she started speaking in tongues. It was so beautiful. It was almost like she was singing. Her speaking in tongues filled me up with such joy that I started shouting, "Alleluia, yes, Jesus, I will be obedient." I just shouted out at the top of my voice, praising Him, chanting "alleluia" over and over again, and that I would be obedient. It seemed like I was given instructions on a deeper level than human. It was as if Jesus gave me instructions directly to my soul by passing the human aspects of my body. It was so beautiful. God was answering my prayers so quickly. I could hardly believe it. Pure love is so strong; you can hardly take it in at one time. I learned that my prayer partner also has special gifts. She also reads the Bible, which is something that I am trying to learn how to do more effectively.

Week 2, Day 2: Sunday, October 4, 2009

While we see the disharmony, strife, and division on this earth, Jesus Christ is pure love. I was so humbly able to experience only a small taste of how wonderful love can be when my prayer partner spoke in tongues over the phone to me yesterday. The love radiated through the phone. It was beautiful—I can still feel the love that I felt. I cannot describe in words how beautiful and loving I felt. It was as if I was bestowed with a gift for a mission I have to do down here on earth.

"There is one Lord, one faith, one baptism, one God, and Father of all, who is over all, and works through all, and is in all" (Eph. 4:5, 6).

Good morning, dear Jesus. Do you have anything to say today? I would love and would be humbly honored to hear from you.

Yes. You are coming along just fine. Keep doing what you are doing. The time is coming near and you are prepared. Watch people in the group. Look at them—you will begin to be able to see their souls, to see who they really are. You will see the good and the bad. The bad (evil) you should be concerned about. They are lurking among our people trying to destroy them. We cannot have that happen. We must do something about it. You are a soldier of God. You will help to destroy evil and you will. You are strong. No evil can be bestowed upon you. You belong to God. You are my soldier. You will be all powerful. Use it wisely. And you will. You are faithful; you are pure in spirit. Your desire is to help people and you will. Go in peace.

Thank you, Jesus.

***

Here are the thoughts I had throughout day two of the seminar:

This morning at 10:06 a.m., I was getting dressed, and as I looked in the mirror, a thought came to me that I am a soldier of God.

I became excited; chills came all over my body the same way when I was praising the Lord when my prayer partner spoke in tongues over the phone. I started jumping up and down praising the Lord saying over and over again, "I am a soldier of God, alleluia, alleluia! Yes, I will be obedient." It went on for several minutes. It was beautiful.

Week 2, Day 3: Monday, October 5, 2009

Abba (Father). We are heirs to God and Jesus Christ. We are family. We have a bloodline directly to Jesus Christ and God. Isn't that wonderful? We are loved. We are never alone. We have our Father above and our Brother Jesus. I so love you Jesus and our heavenly Father above.

"You did not receive a spirit of slavery leading you back into fear, but a spirit of adoption through which we cry out, 'Abba!' The Spirit himself gives witness with our spirit that we are children of God. But if we are children, we are heirs as well: heirs of God, heirs with Christ, if we suffer with him so as to be glorified with him" (Rom. 8:15–17).

Good morning, Jesus, my Brother. Do you have something to tell me this morning? I am so happy to be your sister. Actually, I am honored Jesus, my Lord, God, and Savior. Dear Jesus, I do love you. I am learning so much.

You are faithful. You are doing what I am asking of you. Stay faithful to the Word. You will not perish. You will live forever. I am asking you to do something that will take up some of your time, but you will be able to accomplish everything. So don't worry about being able to finish every chore you may have to do. Life is not easy but challenging. That is why you are on earth. Life is full of challenges, but you will be able to accomplish them. Have faith, be patient. The time is coming near. You will know when the time is right. All of us are family. We belong together, and we all will be together soon. Stay faithful. God is at your side. No harm will befall you. God is protecting you. You will protect others. It is your destiny to protect others. I will show you how to protect them. It is coming soon. Be obedient and God will reward you. Go now and wait for day three.

Jesus, you said wait for day three. This is day three. What does that mean?

Some things will happen today. You will be able to overcome them. It is not harmful. You will be pleased. Wait for the day to unfold. I am pleased that you did not doubt me, but I knew that you did not understand what was being said. Good child, you are truly believing in me. Go in peace and wait for day four.

Thank you, Jesus.

Week 2, Day 4: Tuesday, October 6, 2009

Oh, Jesus, I am honored that you chose me. I had the opportunity to have a taste of true love and it is beautiful when my prayer partner spoke in tongues. Thank you, Jesus. Thank you so much.

"It was not you who chose me. It was I who chose you to go forth and bear fruit. Your fruit must endure, so that all you ask the Father in my name he will give you" (John 15:16).

Good morning, dear Jesus. Do you have anything to say today?

Yes. You are doing just fine. Keep moving in the right direction. Your love and admiration of me, your love for me, and your desire to be obedient to me is what I command of you. You are a child of God. No one will harm you. You are protected. You have responsibilities to the Lord. You have a divine mission to the Lord. You will rise up and protect many people. You are an archangel of God. You will command evil to leave and it will, for evil is afraid of you and rightfully so. You are the chosen one. You will be obedient and follow my instructions. Go now and wait for day five.

Thank you, Jesus.

Week 2, Day 5: Wednesday, October 7, 2009

God wants all people to find oneness and peace with Him. God will not give up on any of His children. Oh, Jesus, I am so happy to find oneness with you and to be at peace with my spirit, my soul.

Good morning, Jesus, do you have anything to say this morning?

Yes, I do. You are the chosen one. Don't let other people get in the way of your divine path. You do not have to impress anyone. Be your own person. People who you need to come in contact with will happen naturally. Do not be afraid. Everything is going as planned. Keep going. You are going in the right direction. Keep the faith and you will be fine. Continue to read the Bible. There is no mistake. You are where you are supposed to be. Go now and wait for day six.

Thank you, Jesus.

Week 2, Day 6: Thursday, October 8, 2009

"Whatever you do, whether in speech or in action, do it in the name of the Lord Jesus. Give thanks to God the Father through him" (Col. 3:17).

It is very hard to try to break old habits. With your help, dear Jesus, I will be able to treat everyone as if I am talking to you.

Dear Jesus, do you have anything to say today?

Yes. Go in peace, my child. Do not worry about anything. You are a child of God. You will not be harmed in any way including in finances, health, and love for your fellow man. You will be able to overcome any obstacle that comes your way. Stay faithful. Everything is going to be all right. Go in peace and wait for day seven.

Thank you, Jesus.

Week 2, Day 7: Friday, October 9, 2009

I now know that trusting in God gives me a sigh of relief that everything is going to be all right. Through the Grace of God, I have raised three kids on my own, I own a condo, drive a nice car, and I have a job that I love as a community college associate professor, all through the Grace of God. When you have troubles on your mind, lean on Jesus. He will get you through every time. When troubled, know that, "and this too shall pass." Thank you, Jesus, for loving me and protecting me. I love you so much.

"Only in God be at rest, my soul, for from him comes hope. He only is my rock and my salvation, my stronghold; I shall not be disturbed. With God is my safety and my glory, he is the rock of my strength; my refuge is in God. Trust in Him at all times, O my people! Pour out your hearts before him; God is our refuge!" (Ps. 62:6–9).

Good morning, dear Jesus. Do you have anything to say this morning?

Yes. You are doing well. You are doing what I ask of you. You are being obedient. Keep moving in the right direction. Everything is going to be all right. Keep the faith. Know that I will provide for you. You shall not perish. You belong in heaven sitting at the right hand of the Father along with Jesus. Go now and wait for day one.

Thank you, Jesus.

***

Here are my thoughts on day seven of week two.

After re-reading what Jesus told me this morning, I asked, "Are you Jesus speaking to me?"

Yes, I am. I speak in your language for you to understand.

Thank you, Jesus.

In week two, I experienced an evil spiritual entity. I had the experience one night as I went to sleep something held me down with the feeling of a pillow over my face. I rebuked in the name of Jesus. It suddenly like it came, let me go. I knew then Jesus is all powerful. I know I can call on him and Jesus will protect me. Jesus will protect you too. Some of you may have similar experiences or know of someone who has similar experiences.

I also realized this week that I was a soldier of God and I will be dealing with spiritual warfare. Part of my destiny is to protect others. Jesus revealed to me that I would be casting out demons. He told me that evil will be afraid of me.

Jesus told me that I was the chosen one. I so humbly accept my assignment. Jesus told me that I would speak to groups and give messages for His people, which I have done since the seminar.

What was fascinating to me was when Jesus told me that I was an archangel. He told me that I will command evil to go and it will. I did not ask Jesus for this assignment. He gave it to me and you must accept yours. It may not be what you prayed for and maybe it will be, but whatever the Lord gives you, accept your spiritual gifts from Him. In week two, I know I can communicate to Jesus because He also told me that He speaks in our own language and I understand Him. Stop, be quiet, and ask for the Holy Spirit to speak to you, and the Holy Spirit will. This has been such a revealing week two. I am ready for week three.

Chapter 3

Week 3: Wholesomeness in Love

"He himself bore our sins in his body upon his cross, so that, free from sin, we might live for righteousness. By the wounds you have been healed" (1 Peter 2:24)

At the seminar on Friday night, October 9, 2009, there was a question for the group breakout sessions: How have you experienced God's healing? Going to the seminar this evening was quite interesting. I found out that other people had similar experience to me, and that Jesus had blessings for all of us if we were willing to accept them.

One woman had severe back pains and took a lot of pain medication. She liked to fast on Mondays, but it was hard to fast because she needed to take her medication with her meals. So one Monday she prayed to God to take away her pain. She no longer has any pain. She informed us that although the doctors said the physical diagnoses were the same and she should still have severe pain, she didn't. She no longer walked with a limp because she was now pain free.

I told the experience I'd had with my gums. I had a hereditary gum disease where eventually I could lose all of my teeth. My mother had to have all her teeth pulled in her later years of life. In 2005, I had surgery on my gums of which one of my teeth could not be saved and the dentist had to pull it. After surgery, I had to go in every three months for teeth cleaning with intervals of gum treatment with the cleaning.

After a year, the dentist who did surgery on my gums performed a follow-up exam and x-rayed my entire mouth. He was amazed that my teeth were still strongly attached to my gums. One tooth that he was watching closely was still intact. The dentist leaned over and whispered in my ear, "What did you do?" I told him he was a good surgeon and that I'd followed all of his instructions.

When I told my sister, she said, "Don't you remember? We went to a healing mass." I had forgotten about the healing mass. To this day, my teeth bleed very little when I get them cleaned, and the gums are strongly attached to my teeth. Miracles are happening to us all the time, but sometimes we don't realize or recognize them even when we specifically ask for them.

There were others in the seminar who had similar experiences. One man had gone to the Lourdes water in France to bathe where people were healed from the holy water. The holy water flows from a spring in the Grotto of Massabielle in the Sanctuary of Our Lady of Lourdes. This man went because he said when he was young his aunt was very mean to him. She'd contracted cancer and he went to the Lourdes water to help her. He said he bathed and when he got out, he was not given a towel. As he began putting on his clothes, a warm feeling came over him. He noticed that he was dry while putting on his clothes although he didn't use a towel. He said when he returned home, his aunt changed and began treating him very nice.

It was interesting to hear how people's experiences were in some ways similar my own. You begin to realize that you are not all alone in these spiritual experiences.

One of the important things I got out of this week was reading the Bible. How often do you read the Bible? I feel spiritual and glorified when I read God's words directly out of the Bible.

I also learned that if we understand love, we will be able to forgive. You do not forgive a person if you still hold anger and resentment toward that person. Forgiveness makes you sick. Love heals.

This week's lesson taught me to understand that everyone has his or her own divine path to follow. They have their own destiny, including our children. My adult children need to make decisions for themselves. It is not for me to control their adult lives.

Jesus reminded me to stay on track—to be obedient, faithful, and stay on my divine path. He gave me my first assignment in the seminar in week three, day four. My assignment was to talk to as many participants in the seminar as possible. I was to stay at the end of the meeting and socialize with the group. Prior to this time, I would go home right after the meeting was over. I followed Jesus' command and I stayed afterwards and socialized with the group

The following are my journal entries over the course of seven days in week three.

Week 3, Day 1: Saturday, October 10, 2009

It is a wonderful feeling that Jesus loves us and forgives us. Thank you, Jesus, for dying on the cross for us. Through your sacrifice, we will be saved.

Healing takes place with forgiving others, not holding resentment, anger, or bad feelings toward other people. These things make us sick because it goes against love. If we truly love, we would be able to forgive. We must learn to truly love our fellow people, our brothers and sisters of the world.

". . . and forgive us the wrong we have done as we forgive those who wrong us" (Matt. 6:12).

Good morning, Jesus. Do you have anything to say?

Yes. You are doing great. You are beginning to understand the true meaning of love. You will soon begin to love your fellow brothers and sisters in a more meaningful way. Keep moving in the right direction. Purchase your Bible. You must read the Bible more. You will understand shortly what I mean. Go now and wait for day two.

Thank you, Jesus.

Week 3, Day 2: Sunday, October 12, 2009

Jesus Christ has the power to heal us and forgive our sins. As we draw near Him, we must ask for forgiveness. Ask Him to heal us.

"In his own body, he brought your sins to the cross, so that all of us dead to sin, could live in accord with God's will. By his wounds you were healed" (1 Pet. 2:24).

God morning, dear Jesus, do you have anything to say?

Yes. You must not get discouraged. Everything is going to be all right. Your oldest child is doing well. She is going to get through this. It is not of your concern. You must stay focused on your own divine path. Do not waste time worrying about her or any of your children. They're fine. They are also strong in the Lord. They will be able to overcome their obstacles in life. They must live their own divine paths the same way you have to. So go in peace.

Thank you, dear Jesus. I guess I had begun to worry about my oldest daughter without realizing it fully, but I know I must trust in you. You have told me before and I am sorry to start to worry again.

Please help me to learn not to worry. I love you so much and yet sometimes my heart gets a little low. Thank you for my divine path. I am already beginning to feel better as I speak to you.

Please continue to heal me in body, spirit, and soul. I love you, dear Jesus. You are my best friend, my brother, my Lord. Thank you for everything because it is through you that I am being saved. Thank you for choosing me. I will obey. I will not let you down.

Week 3, Day 3: Monday, October 12, 2009

We all need to know that we need to ask for forgiveness from Jesus. I need to acknowledge that I have sinned and for Jesus to forgive me. Only then can I be saved.

"Jesus said to them, 'The healthy do not need a doctor, sick people do. I have not come to invite the self-righteous to a change of heart, but sinners'" (Luke 5:31–32).

Good morning, Jesus. Do you have anything to say?

Yes. You are doing well. Keep going in the right direction. Everything is going to be all right with your son and all of your children. Let go of worry. You can do it. You are on a mission, so you cannot get bogged down with trivial thoughts. There's a lot to do. You have a heavy burden of commitment from me. You will understand later. Just keep going. Keep reading the Bible with your prayer partner. Your prayer partner also has a mission, a divine path, but it is different from yours. Go in peace and wait for day four.

Thank you, Jesus.

Week 3, Day 4: Tuesday, October 13, 2009

Jesus gave me my first assignment in the seminar group. My assignment was to talk to as many participants in the seminar as possible. I was to stay at the end of the meeting and socialize with the group. Prior to this time, I would go home right after the meeting was over. I followed Jesus' command and I stayed afterward and socialized with the group.

I do feel an inner freedom believing and trusting in Jesus.

"There is no condemnation now for those who are in Christ Jesus. The law of the spirit, the spirit of life in Christ Jesus, has freed you from the law of sin and death" (Rom. 8:1–2).

Good morning, Jesus. Do you have anything to say?

Yes. Go now and begin to teach the word to people. Tell them that God is real and is coming one day. They will listen to you, for you will have an aura about you and people will know that you are special. You will do this on Friday with the seminar group. Talk to as many individuals as you can. Stay and socialize with them. They do want to talk to you, but they do not get the chance. You will be receptive to them. Go now in peace.

Thank you, Jesus.

Week 3, Day 5: Wednesday, October 14, 2009

I ask for forgiveness, Jesus, and to forgive my family, friends, and the world. I need to learn not to judge others or expect them to behave a certain way just because I feel it is the way to behave. Everyone has their reasons why they do what they do. Please forgive us, Jesus. Please heal us.

"Hence, declare your sins to one another, and pray for one another, that that you may find healing" (James 5:16).

Good morning, Jesus. Do you have anything to say?

Yes. You will be all right. Stay focused and on track to your divine path. Do not let anything get in the way of what we have to do. You are faithful. Stay faithful. You will be rewarded for your faithfulness. God is watching over you. He knows every move you make. You will be successful. You deserve to be because of your faithfulness. You are honest, kind, and loving to people. You have helped a lot of people and there are many more people for you to help. You will help them in many ways. So stay on track and be obedient to God.

Thank you, dear Jesus. I love you very much. Thank you for your comforting words and wisdom. Thank you, thank you, thank you. I will be obedient. I will be faithful. I will stay on my divine path.

Week 3, Day 6: Thursday, October 15, 2009

I have always known the truth shall set you free. I have said it many times. Now I know this saying comes from the Bible.

"Jesus then went on to say to those Jews who believed in him. 'If you live according to my teaching: you are truly my disciples; then you will know the truth, and the truth will set you free" (John 8:31, 32).

Good morning, dear Jesus. Do you have anything to say?

Yes. You are moving in the right direction. Keep moving. Don't look back. Everything is going to be all right. Do not get depressed. You are doing fine. I know this can be a little over whelming, but trust in me, your Lord, your Savior. The time is getting near. You are to preach the Word to our people. You are a soldier of God. Never let anything get in the way of it. Go now in peace.

Yes, Jesus.

Week 3, Day 7: Friday, October 16, 2009

As I experience the wholeness of God, I feel free, happy, and content. I know God is here for me. He will not let me down. I thank you, Jesus, for guiding me. You give peace and tranquility.

"A clean heart create for me, O God, and a steadfast spirit renew within me" (Ps. 51:12).

Good morning, dear Jesus. Do you have anything to say?

Yes. You are doing fine. Do not worry about anything. You will never have to worry about anything. Be obedient. Stay on track to your divine path. You have work to do today. You will go to the seminar. Speak your mind. Be patient, kind, and courteous even to those you know are evil. Do not let anyone sway you from your divine work. You are strong. You can do it. Stay focused. Stay positive. Do not let anyone get you angry. Remember, we are all God's children. You are happy now.

Thank you, Jesus.

***

I began to read the Bible more in week three. I learned that healing takes place with forgiveness. Jesus taught me to let go of worry. I felt an inner freedom, believing and trusting in Jesus. I gave my commitment to being obedient, faithful, and staying on my divine path in accepting my assignments from Jesus. Jesus encouraged me to trust in Him. He told me I was a soldier of God and to never let anything get in the way of it.

Chapter 4

Week 4: The Helper

"I have baptized you with water;
He will baptize you in the Holy Spirit" (Mark 1:8)

Instead of the Friday evening seminar meeting, we had mass at the church on October 16, 2009. The priest talked about the different gifts that Jesus can bestow upon us. He explained the gift of tongues. A person singing in the choir would speak in tongues at the end of a song. Jesus was letting us know what it sounded like. To my surprise, the priest said that he was going to lay his hands on us this evening so we could receive our gifts. There were two priests to lay hands on us. The priest first prayed that God would give us our gifts and that if there were any evil in us, God would make any evil in us leave.

I found that interesting, because I believed through discernment there was one woman in our group who had evil in her. She just seemed as though she was coming from a dark place. She had hardly looked at me since the second week of the seminar. After the priests laid their hands on us, the woman smiled and looked me in the eyes, which was something she couldn't do before.

There was between thirty-five and fifty of us there from the seminar. After mass, the priest had us to sit in every other row. One of the priests would come behind us in the empty row, lay his hands on us, and would pray over us individually. I was several rows back. As I waited anxiously, I prayed and thanked Jesus for giving me this great opportunity to receive all my gifts from Him. I thanked Him for choosing me. I told Him that I would be obedient and do God's will. I was receptive and wanted to be used as a vessel to do God's work.

Finally, the priest came down my row. I took off my glasses because the priest placed both his hands on people's eyes and forehead. He took his hands and put them on my eyes, and as he prayed, my head began to go backward. As he placed his hands on my forehead, my body became limp. I fell down between the pews with my head still backward. When he stopped, I had to maneuver my knees and my body with the assistance of the woman next to me to get back up into my seat.

It was like I could not have fallen in that position without hurting myself, yet I had no bruises, pain, or soreness getting up and afterwards. I put my face in my hands and just thanked Jesus for this special moment in my life. I knew I was having my gifts confirmed because I knew that Jesus had already chosen me to do God's work.

After mass, I waited around to socialize a little as Jesus instructed. I was glad He told me to stay and talk to people, because I was so excited about what had happened during mass that I would have gone straight to my car and called my prayer partner to tell her of my experience.

Oh, what a wonderful evening. I felt so blessed. I was so lucky to be chosen as one of God's people to do His work. Thank you, Jesus, I love you. I love God, and I love all of my brothers and sister in the universe.

I was obedient. Jesus instructed me to stay after the seminar to socialize with the group. He told me there were participants in the seminar who wanted to speak to me. Oh, thank you, Jesus, for the blessings you gave me that night.

In week four, I was called to follow Jesus' Word. Jesus said that I would be rewarded by God for my obedience. He told me that I understood my mission and I was prepared to carry it out. My relationship with God had grown. I now had communication with God every day in prayer. He said I was the chosen one. I would be happy, and I would be rewarded.

Jesus says, "Do not be afraid." God would protect me. He also said I would re-marry and I would be with the right person. He would allow me to do God's work. I told Jesus that I was not interested in being famous. I was interested in saving souls. If I had a question, Jesus told me not to be afraid to ask Him a question. All throughout week four, Jesus gave me power over evil.

Jesus also gave me several more assignments. He told me to pray every day for those who needed God's help and that they would receive it. Jesus told me who I would help. I was also told that I would go to school and wait for someone to come to me to tell me a problem. I was told not to get emotionally involved. Jesus told me to listen and that I would know what to say and do. Most of all, I could hardly believe that the priest laid hands on me on Friday, and by Sunday, October 18, 2009, I was laying hands on someone.

Here are my journal entries for week four.

Week 4, Day 1: Saturday, October 17, 2009

Now I know I also have the Holy Spirit to help me too. God is a mighty God. We have Jesus and the Holy Spirit to help us. It was John the Baptist who witnessed the role Jesus plays in bringing the Holy Spirit into our lives.

"I have baptized you in water; he will baptize you in the Holy Spirit" (Mark 1:8).

Good morning, dear Jesus. Do you have anything to say?

Yes. You have been blessed by the Holy Spirit. Last night I laid hands on you. You are to go out among the people. Administer the word to our people. You are the chosen one. God will protect you. No evil will come near you for evil is afraid of you and they should be, for God has given you power over evil. Go now and wait for day two.

Thank you, Jesus.

Week 4, Day 2: Sunday, October 18, 2009

"Jesus promised the church leaders that the Holy Spirit would guide them to all truth" (Berardino, 17).

The Holy Spirit can help me too. God is blessing us every day and helping us with the Holy Spirit throughout the day.

Good morning, dear Jesus. Do you have anything to say?

Yes. You are being obedient. You are helping him. He is deeply hurt more than he can express to you. Keep him in your prayers. You will help others the same way, by giving them comfort in a time of need. They will come to you and you will help them. Always keep my teachings in their lives. They will listen to you, for you are the chosen one. Listen to me. Do as I direct you to do. Always remember, I will never tell you to harm anyone. Your gifts are for good not evil. Never use them for evil. You are obedient and I know you will use your gifts for good.

Now you are beginning to use your gifts more precisely with others. You will begin to pray every day for those who needs God's help and that they will receive it. You will be told whom you will help. They may or may not know that they even need the help, but you will know. Today, a person will approach you from church who will need God's help. She will confide in you her troubles. You will lay hands on her and say a prayer to uplift her spirit. At the time, I will tell you the words to say. Do not be afraid that she will not welcome it because she will.

She will immediately feel relief. It will be the beginning of healing her soul. Go now in peace.

Yes, Jesus.

***

Here are the thoughts I had during day two of week four.

I went to 11:00 a.m. mass this morning. As I entered the church, I said good morning to the greeter at the front door. After church, there was an announcement that the seventh-grade class was selling donuts and coffee. I thought it was a good idea because it would be easier for someone to come up to me. So, I purchased two twist donuts and a cup of coffee. I sat down at a table alone so I could wait for someone to come up to me. After a few minutes, the greeter came over to me and sat down. She said, "So you were the one to get the twist donuts." I offered her one of them, but she declined. She had a cherry-filled donut, which was close to what she wanted except for the cherry filling.

The greeter talked about her arthritis. A woman came and sat down near the greeter at the end of the long rectangular table. The woman sat at the end while we sat in the middle across from each other. I was facing the greeter and the woman. Toward the end of the conversation, the woman mentioned needing knee surgery. She also said that the greeter could get surgery for her arthritis. The greeter said she was afraid of anesthesia. She felt that she might not wake up when they put her to sleep. She went on to say that she would be eighty years old in January. The woman said her father had surgery in his eighties and he was now in his nineties.

The woman left and the greeter and I continued talking. She said she was going to the bus stop to go to the newly renovated mall. I knew then that she was the one I would lay hands on. I would have the opportunity to do so before dropping her off at the mall. Therefore, I offered to give her a ride, yet she kindly declined.

I explained to her that the Lord blessed me with a car and He was now blessing her with a ride to the mall. She then felt more comfortable accepting the ride. I told her that I would bring the car around so she wouldn't have to walk far since she used a cane.

As we rode to the mall, we saw the bus and she mentioned she would have missed the bus and would have had to wait for another bus for over thirty minutes because the bus ran slower on Sunday.

I told her that I was taking a seminar on Fridays at the church. I started the conversation, but it shifted to something else. She began talking about the best place to drop her off at the mall. When I pulled into the parking lot, I told her that I had something to tell her. She told me to pull up in the handicap stall because she had a handicap sticker and she wouldn't take that long. So, I did.

I told her once again that I was taking a seminar on Fridays at the church. I told her that the priest had laid hands on the members of the seminar after mass on Friday evening. I mentioned how the priest preached about serving God.

I told her when I was praying this morning that Jesus told me a person was going to come to me and tell me her problems. I was going to lay hands on this person and that the person would welcome it. She immediately said yes. We were holding hands. I let go of one of her hands and placed my right hand on her head. I began to pray over her using her name. I didn't remember what I said, but I did remember that Jesus said not to worry about what to say, for I would know what to say when I was ready to say it. The woman was wearing sunglasses, but she removed them to show me her tears of joy. She thanked me and proceeded to get out of the car.

Wow, I kept thanking Jesus for allowing me to lay hands on someone. This stuff was happening pretty fast! I could hardly believe that the priest had laid his hands on me on Friday and by Sunday I was laying hands on someone else. Thank you, Jesus, for choosing me to be a vessel to help the souls here on earth. In Jesus' name, Amen.

I spoke to my prayer partner briefly, and she gave me several readings from the Bible. My prayer partner always gives me scriptures that were appropriate for the moment. She gave me Jeremiah 23:10–12, 20–22, 33–38 and Mark 7:6–8.

> With adulterers the land is filled; on their account the land mourns, the pasture ranges are scared. Theirs is an evil course, theirs is unjust power. Both prophet and priest are godless! In my very house I find their wickedness, says the Lord, Hence their way shall become for them slippery ground. In the darkness they shall lose their footing, and fall headlong; Evil I will bring upon them: the year of their punishment, says the Lord (Jer. 23:10–12).

> The anger of the Lord shall not abate until he has done and fulfilled what he has determined in his heart. When the time comes, you shall fully understand. I did not

send these prophets, yet they prophesied. Had they stood in my council, and did they but proclaim to my people my words, they would have brought them back from all evil ways and from their wicked deeds (Jer. 23: 20–22).

And when this people or a prophet or a priest asks you, 'What is the burden of the Lord?' you shall answer, 'You are the burden, and I can cast you off, says the Lord. If a prophet or a priest or anyone else mentions the burden of the Lord, I will punish that man and his house. Thus you shall ask, when speaking to one another, 'What answer did the Lord give?' Or, 'What did the Lord say?' But the burden of the Lord you shall mention no more. For each man has his own word becomes the burden so that you pervert the words of the living God, he Lord of hosts, our God. Thus shall you ask the prophet, 'What answer did the Lord give?' or, 'What did the Lord say? But if you ask about the burden of the Lord, then thus says the Lord: Because you used his phrase, 'the burden of the Lord,' though I forbade you to use it   (Jer. 23:33–38).

He responded, "Well did Isaiah prophesy about you hypocrites, as it is written: This people honors me with their lips, but their hearts are far from me, in vain do they worship me, teaching as doctrines human precepts (Mark 7:6–7).

And now Lord take note of their threats, and enable your servants to speak your word with all boldness, as you stretch forth [your] hand to heal, and signs and wonders are done through the name of your holy servant Jesus (Acts 4:29–30).

Week 4, Day 3: Monday, October 19, 2009

Before going to bed, I was still thinking about how the priests at church seemed to be aloof with me. Usually they were friendlier. I wasn't sure if the priests were just preoccupied or what. After discussing it with my prayer partner, and after reading Psalm 32:8, which says, "I shall . . . give you counsel and watch over you," I talked to Jesus.

Good morning, dear Jesus. May I ask you a question?

I was expecting Jesus to say yes. It was interesting because Jesus just started answering the question without me actually saying the question to Him.

Yes. The priests are not afraid or scared of you. They are not aware of your gifts yet, but soon they will be. The church member will begin to walk without her cane. She will tell many people what happened to her. Many people will come to you for healing. You will only heal those you are instructed to heal. You will be obedient, and you will do as I say. It is okay to speak to people and explain how your gift is to be used. Tell them they must pray to Jesus for healing and if Jesus wants you to heal them you will. Go in peace.

Thank you, Jesus.

I open my life fully to the presence of the Spirit.

"Be filled with the Spirit, addressing one another in psalms and hymns and inspired songs. Sing praise to the Lord with all your heart" (Eph. 5:18–19).

Good morning dear Jesus. Do you have anything to say?

Yes. Everything is coming along just fine. Keep up the good work. You will be rewarded for your good deeds. The day will come when you will have another task. Be patient. Stay on track to your divine path. You are doing a good job. I will be here for you. Do not be afraid to ask me questions. Ask and you shall be answered in Jesus' name. Amen. Go in peace.

Thank you, Jesus.

Week 4, Day 4: Tuesday, October 20, 2009

Thank you, Holy Spirit, for producing and helping me to be touched by God. On Friday, October 16, 2009, I was touched by God again when the priest at church laid hands on me to receive my gifts from God.

"And this hope will not leave us disappointed, because the love of God has been poured out in our hearts through the Holy Spirit who has been given to us" (Rom. 5:5).

Good morning, dear Jesus. Do you have anything to say?

Yes. You will begin another task this morning. You will go to school and wait for someone to come to you and tell you their problems. Listen to them. Do not get emotionally involved in their problem. You will know the words to help them. I will let you know what to say after you listen to them. You will comfort them in a time they will need it the most. Do not be afraid of your work that you are doing for me. You will be rewarded for it. The time is coming for you to begin a larger task with more meaning and depth to it.

Do not be afraid. You are protected from evil. Evil fears you. You can sleep with the light off or on—it doesn't matter. You will always be protected. I know this can be somewhat overwhelming because I am picking up the pace for you to do God's work. You can handle it. You will do just fine. Remember, you must believe in me. You cannot doubt me. I know that you will obey. You are a kind spirit. You have been doing God's work for many years now. God is pleased with your work. Keep it up. Keep moving in the right direction with your divine path. Now go, my child, go in peace.

Thank you, Jesus.

***

Here are the thoughts I had during day four of week four.

This morning one of my students needed my help. He came up to me and said, "It's just my luck—it always happens." The printer wouldn't print out his assignment after class. I thought he was the one I would heal. I told him that things happened to all of us; it was how we responded that was important. When something happened, we needed to learn from it. I told him that he was smart and could be anything he wanted to be in life. He must go to church and pray for Jesus to help him.

I thought my task for Jesus was over. So, I went on my merry way completing my school chores. And then it happened—I passed by my colleague's office quickly, because I saw he was talking to a student. My colleague said, "Hi, Jacki," as I was passing. I stopped and said hi, and he jumped up from his desk to come outside to speak with me for a few minutes. He was sad and seemed to be slightly disappointed. A student had wrongly accused him of something, and the department did not support him.

I knew he was the one that you, Jesus, told me who would come to me for comfort. I listened to him like you told me. I talked to him. I wasn't sure that everything I said to him was from you, but I do remember that he said he felt better after talking to me. I told him that Jesus told me that someone was going to come to me today, and he said he had a feeling that one above was going to speak to him. He thanked me for stopping and talking to him. I could see how relieved he was after our conversation.

Thank you, Jesus, for letting me be a vessel for you. I feel so good inside when I can help someone, especially with the healing of his or her soul. Thank you. Jesus, I love you so very much.

You are being obedient. You are doing what you have been instructed to do. You will continue to help people. Keep up the good work. God will reward you. Go now in peace.

Thank you, Jesus.

Week 4, Day 5: Wednesday, October 21, 2009

I have been called to follow Jesus' directions. I will be obedient. Jesus assured me that I would be rewarded. I felt rewarded when I helped someone heal their soul. Jesus was revealing to me God's gifts to me. I gave messages to people, I have comforted people, and I was also blessed with healing people. Thank you, Jesus, for such wonderful gifts. I will be obedient in Jesus' name, Amen.

". . . The Spirit we have received is not the world's spirit but God's Spirit, helping us to recognize the gifts he has given us" (1 Cor. 2:10–12).

Good morning, dear Jesus. Do you have something to say?

Yes. You are progressing along quite well now. You're getting used to some of your gifts. You have many more to come. You will receive them as you need to administer them. You will be a very famous person in the spirit world. Those who are spiritual will know you well, for you are a leader among the people. They will listen to you in awe, for you have been chosen to help our people of this world.

Lots of work is yet to be done. You are strong and will be able to execute my commands given to you. Stay focused. Stay on your course and destiny for this lifetime. You will be blessed by God Himself, for He loves His children to obey, and you are obedient. You understand your mission here and you are prepared to carry it out. Be patient. Everyone cannot see what you see. Do not be critical of them because they do not have the gifts you have. You are special. Stay the course. Do as you are told, for God will reward you. You will have spiritual friends to share your spiritual successes with. So go now in peace.

Oh, Jesus, I just want to thank you for allowing me to be a vessel to help God's people. I am so grateful and humble to your word. It was very rewarding to me that I was able to help comfort my colleague yesterday. May God be the glory. You used me as a vessel to begin healing the church greeter's soul. Thank you, thank you, thank you, in Jesus' name, Amen.

Week 4, Day 6: Thursday, October 22, 2009

My relationship with the Holy Spirit has grown. My relationship with Jesus has grown. It has grown to a dimension of prayer that we have conversations every day. Thank you, dear Jesus, for your kindness to me.

"But you, beloved, grow strong in your holy faith through prayer in the Holy Spirit" (Jude 1:20).

Good morning, dear Jesus. Do you have anything to say?

Yes. You are doing fine. Keep up the good work. You will begin to have more challenges ahead of you. You will meet people who are in dire need of God's help. You will be able to help them. You will be an inspiration to them. You have special powers that no one else has.

You will be able to heal the sick, fight off evil spirits, and help people who are in need. You have been chosen to do God's work. You will be rewarded for it. You haven't any reasons to be afraid of anything. God will take care of all of your needs. You will be happy. Be patient, my child. Be patient with others.

Remember, everyone cannot see what you see, and cannot do what you do. You are special. You are chosen. Keep doing God's work. You will be rewarded. Stay on track. Do not let people sidetrack you. You will do fine. You will obey. Go now, go in peace.

Thank you, Jesus, for our special time together. I will obey. I love you very much. Thank you for your love and kindness to me. You have blessed me with so much. I do sincerely appreciate all that you have done for me.

Week 4, Day 7: Friday morning, October 23, 2009

I believe in Jesus. I will drink of the Spirit. Please teach me how to be a good person to drink of the Spirit.

"Jesus said that if we drink of the Spirit it will be like rivers of water flowing deep within us" (Berardino, 19).

Good morning, Jesus. Do you have anything to say?

Yes. You are coming along just fine. Keep up the good work for me. You are doing what you are supposed to be doing during this time. Time will come when we will begin to work again. Be patient. Everything will be all right. You will be able to love again, to be with someone again. This time, it will be the right person. He will love you the way you want to be loved and so deserve. You will still do God's work when you remarry. He will be spiritual and will understand. You will have a spiritual connection, which will be different from this world. It will be deeper than this earthly world. You are destined to be famous in the spiritual world. Don't be afraid of it. You will be doing God's work and rightfully so. Go now in peace.

Dear Lord, I am not interested in being famous. I am interested in serving you and in helping people heal their souls. I will obey and do as you instruct me to do. I love you, Jesus, and I thank you for bringing me someone who will truly love me, respect me, and treat me with kindness, as I will love, respect, and treat with kindness.

You are a good person and deserve to be respected and to be happy in life as you go about healing, driving out demons, and restoring health to the soul. You are the chosen one. Some may not know that they need help, but you will know. You will heal, drive out demons, and help restore souls who have gone astray in this earthly place. Be patient. You will soon begin to work on a much deeper level. It is just a matter of time. Let the church member begin to walk, and to spread the word of your gifts from God.

The word is going to spread like wildfire. The priests are going to want to talk to you. They are going to want to know just exactly how you communicate with me and you will tell them. They need to know that everything you are doing is coming from me, your Lord, your God.

It won't be long before you will see the church member walk. She is going to be so happy to see you so she can show you what you did for her. You will remind her that it was not you but Jesus Christ. You are the chosen one. You will do God's will. You will be obedient. Go now in peace and wait for the glory of God.

Thank you, Jesus.

***

Here are my thoughts for day seven of week four.

This morning I called my prayer partner. I talked to her about my morning conversations with Jesus. She always gives me Bible verses to read. We read them. They just come to her while we are talking, and they always reference what is relevant for the day. Sometimes they come to her so fast, I can hardly keep up. This morning she asked me to pray with her to help her heal the back of her left side of her neck and her knees. I prayed with her and then I told her she would need to pray directly to Jesus to ask for healing. I could only heal those that Jesus told me to heal. You must ask Him.

I told her that she would need to overcome fear. She must pray to get rid of fear. I explained that she needed what I call a "trigger" to bring her back on track.

I gave her an example of myself of when Jesus told me to go to the church. He said that someone was going to come up and tell me her problems, and that I was going to lay my hands on her and help her to start healing her soul. Wow, this would be the first person I would have healed.

When I went to church, I was a little nervous, but as soon as doubt crept into my mind, I thought of Peter who walked on water with Jesus. As long as Peter believed, he could walk on the water, but as soon as he looked down and had doubt, he began to sink and Jesus held out His hand to lift him back up.

So, when I thought of Peter, I said, "Yes, Lord, I will obey. Yes, Jesus, I will do as you say over and over until the doubt goes away." So, I told my prayer partner she must have a trigger to help her get rid of fear. The fear would stand in the way of her healing and would give her doubt.

While we were talking, all of a sudden I knew that Jesus gave me permission to heal her. I started shouting, "Thank you, Jesus, for letting me heal my prayer partner. Then I told her that Jesus was going to heal her. I don't know exactly what I said, but I know I mentioned healing the left side of her neck, back, and her knee, ending with in the name of Jesus, Amen.

I was so overwhelmed with joy that tears came to my eyes. I thanked Jesus and kept saying, "alleluia" over and over again. As I was praying to Jesus, my prayer partner starting praying out of the Bible at the same time. She then started speaking in tongues to Jesus. It was so beautiful.

Words cannot describe the experience I had with my prayer partner this morning. I told her that her trigger for fear was "I fear no evil, for I walk in the light of Jesus Christ." While I told her the trigger she would use, I let her know that it was coming from Jesus Christ—I am only the vessel. He used me to give her the message.

Thank you, Jesus, for giving me the honor to be a vessel to give my prayer partner healing this morning. I love you.

In week four, I was called to follow Jesus. I had a commitment with God every day in prayer. My communication had grown. Jesus said, I would be rewarded by God for my obedience. I felt comfortable in praying and listening to Him. He told me not to be afraid. He would protect me and He will protect you too.

This week the priest laid hands on us. After the Friday night mass, the following Sunday, I laid hands on the church greeter for Jesus to heal her so she could walk without her cane. The gifts kept coming to me. Jesus told me to keep praying every day for hope. Jesus gave me several more assignments. He told me to pray for those who need help. He told me to go to school and wait for someone to come to talk about their problems.

Chapter 5

Week 5: Following Jesus

"Then Jesus said to His disciples, 'Who ever wishes to come after me must deny himself, take up his cross and follow me. For whoever wishes to save his life will lose it, but whoever loses his life for My sake will find it . . ." (Matthew 16:24–26)

During Friday night's seminar on October 23, 2009, we started by praising the Lord in song. We prayed one decade of the rosary together. Our guest speaker for the evening spoke on the virtues and the seven gifts of the Holy Spirit. He mentioned several passages from the Bible such as Romans 1 and Isaiah 11:1. He also talked about speaking in tongues. There are different types. Sometime you can speak another language or just sounds.

The priest asked if anyone wanted the gift of speaking in tongues. I raised my hand. To myself, I asked Jesus if he wanted me to speak in tongues. His response was, "So be it." I was never truly drawn to speaking in tongues had and very seldom heard of it. I didn't even know that Catholics spoke in tongues because my only encounters of hearing it before the seminar were people from other Christian religions.

The priest said there were praying tongues and singing tongues. He told us that some people could also interpret tongues. He was going to show us the singing tongues. He had us stand up, and the guitar player played low music in the background as we just said a mantra of alleluia over and over until, if we were given the gift, we would start speaking in tongues.

So, I began repeating "alleluia," and then all of a sudden I started shouting in tongues. My eyes were closed and I felt the priest touch my shoulder and said, "Lower your voice so you can be with the group." I immediately lowered my voice to speak in tongues with the group. I believe I was one of two given the gift of tongues tonight. Praise the Lord!

After we finished, the priest explained why I was shouting in tongues. He said that sometimes when it was your first time speaking in tongues, you shout out, like casting out any demons or old, stressful stuff out of your body. I thanked him for mentioning it in front of the group. The priest was blessed with the Holy Spirit. He was truly a vessel for Jesus.

After speaking in tongues, the priest had us to come up front and sit in the front row so he could lay hands on us while we prayed for our family members. My prayer partner asked me to pray with her for the left side of her neck, lower back, and her knees. I knew she was always praying for the sick so I would pray for her healing tonight.

I went up and quietly waited for the priest to lay his hands on me. I was so excited because I felt so blessed to have another opportunity for someone to lay hands on me. When the priest touched my forehead, my head went back, my eyes were closed, but my eyes were roaming around, and my mouth was wide opened. I prayed for my prayer partner and her healing. I don't know how long I was in that position, but the priest lifted my head and said in a soft voice for me to keep my eyes closed. So I kept praying with my head bent down. It was a beautiful experience.

When we finished for the evening, the prayer leader came over to me to let me know that after the seminar was over in November they would still meet every Friday as a prayer group and offered me the opportunity to continue attending. I thanked her for the opportunity, but I knew Jesus had a mission for me, and I would not know until Jesus gave me direction on which way to go.

She then took my hand and walked me over to the side away from the group that was socializing after the seminar and began to speak in tongues. I joined in and spoke tongues with her. When we finished, she said God wanted her to speak in tongues so that I would.

After we spoke in tongues, I asked the priest if I was ever going to be able to remember how to speak in tongues since it was so new to me. He told me I could practice it in the shower, driving on my way to work, etc. He said I would eventually fit it into my daily prayers or routine of some kind. Before the priest left, I asked him what I was saying, and he said I wasn't speaking a known language—it sounded like gibberish.

Jesus, thank you for the gift of tongues. I had no idea that I would be speaking the gift of tongues tonight. What an honor to speak to you directly. Thank you, Jesus, I love you.

Dear Jesus, do you have anything to say?

Yes. You are getting closer to doing major work for me. You will be given specific instructions on what to do. Do not be afraid. You are protected by me. Go now in peace.

In week five, I received the gift of speaking tongues. I was so elated. Two of my sisters could already speak tongues. I was now the third sister. I made a firm commitment to Jesus that I would obey and do as He commanded of me. I now knew that I was a vessel for Jesus Christ. It was not I, but the Father above. It was Jesus Christ who did all the work.

Jesus told me that I would cast out demons. He also told me that demons would be afraid of me. *Wow,* I thought to myself, *is this really happening to me? Is it happening to anyone else?* I was so happy to have a prayer partner to discuss what was happening with me. I knew that in order to follow Jesus and do as He commanded of me that I would have to give up a part of myself. I would sacrifice to do God's work. Jesus reminded me not to be afraid. He would always be there for me. He also reminded me that He was speaking the language that I understood, and that I should not doubt Him.

Jesus continued to give me assignments. This time I was casting out demons in my student and a minister. The student I laid hands on and spoke in tongues. The minster I spoke in tongues over the telephone. By now I was used to receiving assignments on a regular basis. The readings in Berardino's book, *Thy Kingdom Come,* gave me food for thought for each day.

The following are my journal entries for week five of the seminar.

Week 5, Day 1: Saturday, October 24, 2009

Jesus, I am your follower. I am united with you. I will obey. I am your vessel to bring your word to others and to serve you as you see fit. I love you and I am so happy and humbled to do God's work.

Good morning, dear Jesus. Do you have anything to say?

Yes. Tomorrow is the big day. Everyone is going to know that the church member can walk without her cane. The priest wants to meet you. He wants to know who performed this miracle. He will be surprised that it is you. You are a beautiful woman and do not seem like the one who would perform such a miracle. You will perform many miracles. This is just the beginning of your spiritual journey. Stay focused. Do not let people sidetrack you. You will know what I mean later. You have begun your major spiritual battle. Go now in peace.

Dear Jesus, may I ask you a question?

Yes. I say "battle" because you will also cast out demons. Remember, evil is afraid of you because you are a powerful and mighty spirit. No evil can harm you. Evil fears you because they know you can cast them out. You will cast out evil spirits of those I will command of you to do.

Do not be afraid. You are protected. You are the chosen one. People all over the world are going to want to meet you. Be patient and do as I tell you. You will be famous in the spiritual world. It is your destiny. I know you do not want to be known in the world, but we have work to do. This world is in urgent need of our help. I say "our" because you will be the vessel to do God's work.

You are obedient. You have been for many years now. You have progressed very well over the years. You will pray for people and your prayers will be granted, for you are the chosen one. You will also be able to interpret tongues, which will amaze many people. You are kind and loving. You deserve to be happy and you will be. Remember, I am always watching over you. You are special. Go now in peace.

Thank you, Jesus.

Week 5, Day 2: Sunday, October 25, 2009

Today is a very good daily reminder of Jesus for me. I know today I will see the church member walk. I have taken up the cross for

Jesus many years ago, but now it becomes a little heavier. I am asked to do more for Jesus and I will obey. I know my life will change from this day forward.

"We cannot follow Jesus very far if we fail to take up our cross" (Berardino, 23).

I understand that I will have to give up myself to follow Jesus. I understand now why I must be famous in the spiritual world. It is not for me, but for Jesus' word to spread among His people. I know today is the beginning of spreading Jesus' word to many people and for many people to come.

"Then Jesus said to His disciples, 'Who ever wishes to come after me must deny himself, take up his cross and follow me. For whoever wishes to save his life will lose it, but whoever loses his life for My sake will find it . . .'" (Matt. 16:24–26).

Good morning, Jesus. Do you have anything to say?

Yes. You are progressing well. You are obeying. You are doing what you are told to do. You will be rewarded for it. Keep moving in the right direction. Today is a big day. Yes, your life will begin to change from this day forward. Don't be afraid. I will always be there for you. I will protect you. No evil can bestow itself upon you. I have spoken. Go in peace.

Thank you, Jesus.

Right after mass, I waited to see the church member. I realized that Jesus did not say I was going to meet her. I think I made some assumptions on my part. I finished eating my donut after mass, but I didn't see the church member. I asked Jesus if I could ask Him a question because I needed to know if she was here today and if I could leave. Jesus answered.

Yes, you can leave. She is not here today, but she has already spread the news. They are waiting to meet you.

Dear Jesus, may I ask a question?

Yes. The work has begun. Everyone knows about the miracle. They just don't know who performed the miracle yet, but they will. Be patient, my dear. They are wondering who it could be. The church members will meet you soon. They are trying to figure out how they can meet you as soon as possible. They know mass has ended so they do not have any idea. Don't worry. They will meet you soon. Wait until tomorrow. Something unusual will happen, nothing to alarm you. Just wait until tomorrow. Do not doubt me. Stay on track. I know you will obey. Now go and wait for day three.

Dear Jesus, may I ask you another question?

Yes. Do not worry about how I tell you. I am speaking the language that you understand. Things are beginning to go faster with you. You need to be alert. Things will come your way. You have to be ready when they come. Do not doubt me, because everything is going along as planned. Go in peace.

Yes, Jesus.

Week 5, Day 3: Monday, October 26, 2009

I do truly believe that everything in our lives that did not come from God loses its meaning. This earthly material stuff is not why we are here. We are here to develop our spirituality. Things that came from God (our faith, families, etc.) will acquire greater meaning than this earthly place and its materials in it. I also believe that Jesus Christ is our greatest treasure. I was just talking to my brother last night about our true meaning for being here on this earth to develop our spirituality.

Good morning, dear Jesus. Do you have anything to say?

Yes. You are doing great. You have obeyed me. You are sad this morning. Do not be sad or disappointed. Everything is going to be all right. Everything is falling into place as planned. You are the chosen one. People already know about the miracle that took place with the church member. I know it is a bit of a letdown from yesterday. Let us not spend any more time or energy thinking about it. You have work to do.

Today you will need to be aware of surroundings. People are not who they think they are. They don't even really know themselves. Evil may lurk in a body when the person may not even know it. You are to cast out evil today.

You will meet someone who is entrapped with an evil spirit. He will want you to help him. He is in your class at school. He is going to come to you to talk about his troubles. You are to lay your hands on him and cast out the evil spirit. You do not have to worry because the evil spirit is afraid of you and your powers. It will leave quickly.

Your student will thank you for helping him, for setting him free. You can see his face as we speak. He has dark hair. That's the one. He is very soft-spoken in class. He cannot focus in class because of this evil spirit. After you cast it out, he will be able to become an A student. Go now. Go in peace, my child. I have spoken.

Dear Jesus, may I ask you a question?

Yes. The minister needs your help. Call him right now and pray the gift of tongues with him on the phone. I have spoken.

Dear Jesus, may I ask a question?

Yes. You need to call again. This time he will answer. I have spoken.

Dear Jesus, may I ask you a question?

Yes. He is there. You must keep trying. Call his home number. Do not leave a message. Just keep calling until he answers. I have spoken. He will answer. He needs your help.

Thank you, Jesus, for allowing me to be your vessel to help the minister. He answered the phone and I prayed the gift of tongues with him. He prayed while I spoke in tongues. I remembered that I waved my arm away from my body, saying, "It's gone, it's gone—you can do your work." I told the minister Jesus said he would know what it means. I spoke again in tongues and then told him good-bye and hung up.

Dear Jesus, may I ask you a question?

Yes. Yes, you cast out a demon in the minister. The minister has been praying to be released from it and he is. You will work with other ministers the same way. They will be ever so grateful for your help.

They will not be able to do it alone. I will tell you from whom I want to drive out demons. The ministry world will know you for this gift. The minister is just the first one you have helped. You can do it in person, over the phone, and through prayer.

Thank you, Jesus, for using me to do God's work. I am only your vessel. I know that not I, but you, Jesus, and the Father above, are performing these miracles and casting out demons. Thank you, Jesus, for such an honor.

After I laid my hands on a student to drive out a demon, I asked Jesus:

Dear Jesus, may I ask you a question?

Yes. You did a great job. You will be able to tell how well you did when he returns on Wednesday. He knows that you helped him. He knew right after you did it. Make sure when the opportunity presents itself—and you will know when that is—to tell him that it was Jesus answering his prayers. Go now in peace.

Yes, Jesus.

Week 5, Day 4: Tuesday, October 27, 2009

When you really get it, you know this earthly ". . . world can throw many negative, ungodly influences at us but when we embrace the cross of our Lord Jesus Christ these forces lose their power over us" (Berardino, 24).

"May I never boast of anything but the cross of our Lord Jesus Christ!" (Gal. 6:14).

Good morning, dear Jesus. Do you have anything to say?

Yes. You are doing a good job. You are obedient and doing what you are supposed to do. You have another task for today. You will see a friend you have not seen in a long time. She is very troubled and needs you to comfort her. She is going to bump into you at a store. It won't be a long encounter, but long enough to know she is deeply troubled and needs spiritual help. You will cast out a demon in her later, not today. The opportunity will come for you to do so. Just remember, when you see her again, you will need to cast out the demon. She will be receptive to it. Go now in peace.

Thank you, Jesus.

Week 5, Day 5: Wednesday, October 28, 2009

There is a lot of injustice in this world. I do choose to obey and follow Jesus knowing that I have found great purpose and fulfillment in doing so.

Good morning, dear Jesus. Do you have anything to say?

Yes. You are progressing along well, my child. Keep up the good work. You are obeying my words and direction. You will have other tasks to do. Soon you will meet the priest of the parish. He is dying to see you. He can't wait to see who performed this miracle. They are waiting in anticipation as to what you will do next. You will tell them that you are doing God's work. Whatever I say you will do. If they need something, they must pray to me and I will let them know if I am to heal them.

Friday evening will be another interesting night. There will be a lot of people there to hear the priest speak so get there early. You are to sit up in the first row, for something special will occur. You will be all right. You are doing fine.

I know you are amazed at what you are doing for God's people. Helping people makes you feel so good inside. That is why I chose you. You have a pure spirit of love and understanding of the people. You feel what they feel. You help them as though they are in your immediate family.

I wonder what happened to the friend I haven't seen in a long time. I never bumped into her in the store.

Dear Jesus, may I ask you a question?

Yes. You will meet this person soon. When you do, you will know she is the one I am talking about. It will happen soon. Now go, child, go in peace.

Thank you, Jesus.

Dear Jesus, may I ask another question?

Yes. It was not her. You have not encountered her yet. Go in peace.

Thank you, Jesus, for the wonderful conversation we had this morning. I feel that I can now talk to you at will. Thank you so very much for choosing me and choosing my prayer partner. You have also given her great spiritual gifts. I will obey. We will obey. I will do your will, dear Lord. Thank you, thank you, thank you.

***

Hello, Jesus. I talked to the student today after class and told him Jesus answered his prayer. I asked him if he knew what I was talking about and he said yes. He seemed more content in class than ever before. Thank you, Jesus, for allowing me to be the vessel to answer the student's prayer in driving out the demon.

Do you have anything to say, dear Jesus?

Yes, a job well done. You are obeying God's will. You will continue to do God's will. There are many people in need of spiritual healing. You will help many people. Stay the course. Everything is going as planned. It won't be long before you meet your husband. Yes, husband. You will marry again. This time it will be for all the right reasons. Hold on. You are going to be very happy again.

Time is coming near to begin work again. It will be with your church. They already have an idea that you are special and have special gifts in your Friday group. They are right. You do, but you already know that. Stay the course. Everything is going to be all right with you and your kids.

You have chosen a very special person for your prayer partner. She will help you in your journey, and she is very happy to be your prayer partner. You two are very close, and you should be because there is a lot of work to do.

In your vision, you saw her standing side by side with you because the both of you work together sometimes. You have different gifts that complement each other. So, stay the course. Go now. Go in peace.

Yes, Jesus.

Week 5, Day 6: Thursday, October 29, 2009

Oh, dear Jesus, you have given me strength in my faith and in taking care of all of my needs.

"God promises to deliver those who are just from all their troubles. When we put our faith in God's promise, we will be strengthened by the hope we need" (Berardino, 25).

Good morning, dear Jesus. Do you have anything to say?

Yes. You will begin your work again. Soon you will meet the person of your dreams. He is handsome, smart, rich, kind, loving, and of course spiritual. You deserve a good person in your life that understands you and will give you the nurturing that you need. Don't be afraid to love again. You are doing earthly things, as well as spiritual things, in this lifetime. So, stand strong and be brave. Remember, I will always be with you. You are never alone. Go now. Go in peace.

Thank you, dear Jesus. I am so appreciative for all that you do for me. Thank you, thank you, thank you.

Week 5, Day 7: Friday, October 30, 2009

I feel as I get closer to you, Jesus, I have a whole new life. I do not worry anymore because I know you are by my side. Thank you,

Jesus, for choosing me. Oh, Jesus, I love you so much. Thank you for all that you have done for me.

Good morning, dear Jesus. Do you have anything to say today?

Yes. Today is a big day. Something very special is going to happen tonight. Remember, you must be early and sit in the front row. God has spoken. Go in peace.

Dear Jesus, may I ask you a question?

Yes. You will need to read a book called, You Will be Made up of Armor to Kill. *It will give you an idea of what spiritual warfare is all about. Driving out demons is only one of many gifts you will receive. You will be able to interpret any kind of tongues you can hear. You will not be limited to only interpreting your own tongues. You will interpret all tongues. You will work with many different people because you will multitask. You are doing as you are told. Keep up the good work. Go now. Go in peace.*

Thank you, Jesus.

***

In week five, Jesus told me to read a book called, *You Will be Made up of Armor to Kill* but I could not find it. I eventually read a Spiritual Warfare Handbook.

Also in this week, I received another spiritual gift, the gift of tongues. One of my sisters is my prayer partner and she was already speaking tongues. She spoke tongues before I could. I also have two other sisters that were already speaking tongues. There are four of us in my family who can speak tongues. I have five sisters and two brothers. This was amazing to me. God is so good.

Jesus also let me know that I would be speaking to groups with messages for his people. I now deliver messages in my parish charismatic prayer group. He mentioned again that I was the chosen one. I also realized that I was a soldier of God dealing with spiritual warfare. I learned that it was my destiny to protect others. He mentioned to me that evil would be afraid of me. Jesus often repeated these things to me. I guess I needed to hear them that many times. So much was happening to me. I know it has happened to others and if it has not already happening to you, receiving spiritual gifts can happen to you too. I know more is to come. I graciously waited for week six.

Chapter 6

Week 6: The Fruit of the Spirit

"... In contrast, the fruit of the spirit is love, joy, peace, patience, kindness, generosity, faithfulness, gentleness, self-control..." (Galatians 5:22)

Jesus expressed to me that I was doing well as His vessel. However, one important thing that I learned this week was that Jesus' prophecy did not always happen within the time frame that I thought it would happen. I have to remember that it was God's time and with the willingness of the person involved. It was done unto you as you believed.

"And Jesus said to the centurion, 'you may go; as you have believed, let it be done for you.' And at that very hour [his] servant was healed" (Matt. 8:13).

"When he entered the house, the blind men approached him and Jesus said to them, 'do you believe that I can do this?' 'Yes, Lord,' they said to him. Then he touched their eyes and said. 'Let it be done for you according to your faith" (Matt. 9:28–29).

People have free will to make decisions.

During week six, I felt good as I walked in the light of Jesus Christ. Jesus reminded me as I served Him, that I was to be strong and stay strong. He also told me that I was from a bloodline of spiritual people, saints, and holy people. What an honor to hear this from Jesus.

Also during this week, I realized that at some point in my life I would lose the freedom of the quietness of not being in the public's eye, so to speak. It was a very sad moment for me, yet I felt very happy to have such a special relationship with Jesus Christ.

Below are my journal entries for week six.

Week 6, Day 1: Saturday, October 31, 2009

Dear Jesus, I will abide in an on-going relationship with you, my Lord and Savior.

Good morning, dear Jesus. Do you have anything to say?

Yes. You are doing well. You are obedient. You will be rewarded for it. Stay the course. Continue what you are doing. Everything is going according to plan. Go now. Go in peace.

Thank you, Jesus.

Week 6, Day 2: Sunday, November 1, 2009

Thank you, Jesus, for rooting in me the temperament that God originally created us to be.

> I say, then: live by the Spirit and you will certainty not gratify the desire of the flesh. For the flesh has desire against the Spirit, and the Spirit against the flesh; these are opposed to each other, so you may not do what you want. But if you are guided by the Spirit, you are not under the law. Now the works of the flesh are obvious: immorality, impurity, licentiousness, idolatry, sorcery, hatreds, rivalry, jealousy, outbursts of fury, and acts of selfishness, dissensions, factions, and occasion of envy, drinking bouts, orgies, and the like. I warn you, as I warned you before, that those who do such things will not inherit the kingdom of God. In contrast, the fruit of the spirit is love, joy, peace, patience, kindness, generosity, faithfulness, gentleness, self-control. Against such there is no law (Gal. 5:16–23).

Good morning, dear Jesus. Do you have anything to say?

Yes. Keep doing what you are doing. Everything is going along as planned. You will encounter a church member today. She has told everyone who would listen about her miracle to be able to walk without her cane. You will meet the priest. He is going to be so surprised to know that it was you. He has seen you around the parish for years now but did not have a clue that it would be you to perform this miracle. He is going to want to talk to you and hear all the details of your miracle. You may tell him that it was I, not you, which he will already know. Don't be afraid of all the attention that you will get. You deserve it. I know that you will keep everything in perspective and continue to let people know that it is me not you. You will obey. You are a good servant of God. You are humble, kind, loving, and deserving of a good life. Go now in peace.

Thank you, Jesus.

***

Here are my thoughts throughout day one of week six.

I went to the 11:00 a.m. Sunday mass. I saw the church member sitting at the door greeting us as we entered the church. She told me that she had the flu last week and was very sick. That's why she wasn't able to come to church. She asked if I missed her, and I told her that I did. I was so used to her greeting us at the door.

I saw her cane leaning against the wall. I figured she was still using the cane. I went into church. I was a little confused, but Jesus told me to have faith and I told Him I did. I knew everything happened on Jesus's time, not mine. After church, the church member came up to me. I asked her if she needed a ride. She said she was going back to the mall to return some pants. At first I said that I would drive her, but I remembered that some furniture was being delivered to my house between 1:00 and 4:00 p.m., so I told her I could take her to the bus stop. She said that would be wonderful.

While driving to the bus stop, I asked the church member how her walking was coming along. I just said whatever came into my head. She said that she would always use a cane and that she would not be able to walk without it. She mentioned before that it was also painful to walk. She has prayed a lot, even to St. Jude. Just before getting out of the car, I said something about Jesus to her, but I don't remember. When she started getting out of the car, I told her that she would be walking soon. She said, "I sure do hope so." She said it with little conviction in her voice. Then she looked hopeful.

Dear Jesus, may I ask you a question?

Yes. Be patient. The time is near. You told her today that she would walk very soon. She responded with doubt of it happening, with little hope that she could. She will walk today at the mall. She is going to start walking at first, not realizing that she is not using her cane. She is going to call the priest at church right away. He is going to call you. He can't wait to hear what you have to say. Just remember to say, "It is not I but the Father above." It is going to happen today. Just be patient. This is a big day today. Go in peace.

Thank you, Jesus. I know that I need not anticipate anything but to wait for it to unfold.

I called to talk to my prayer partner to discuss today's events. We talked for a few minutes discussing expectations. She had to go to the store and said she would call me right back. As I waited for her call, I started speaking in tongues. I started with low energy and then all of a sudden a burst of energy came forth and I knew Jesus had performed His miracle on the church member. This was a little after 2:00 p.m. I began speaking in tongues as if I was giving Glory to God for the miracle He had performed. My prayer partner called back and I told her what happened, and then a burst of energy while speaking tongues blurted out again while my prayer partner was on the phone. She prayed while I spoke in tongues.

Week 6, Day 3: Monday, November 2, 2009

It is so true that happiness comes to us when we walk in the light of the Lord and bear spiritual fruit. So many good things has happened to me by following and obeying Jesus. Thank you, Jesus, for choosing me and allowing me to walk in the light of you in a very special way. Thank you, thank you, thank you.

"Happy are those who do not follow the counsel of the wicked, nor go the way of sinners, nor sit in company with scoffers. Rather, the law of the Lord is their joy; God's law they study day and night. They are like a tree planted near streams of water that yields its fruit in season; its leaves never wither; whatever they do prospers" (Ps. 1:1–3).

Good morning, dear Jesus. Do you have something to say?

Yes. You are progressing. You are beginning to understand how everything works. You are right. Do not anticipate—just let it unfold. I will never lead you astray. You must have faith. You must believe and you will. You are obedient. You are doing what you are told to do. You will be rewarded. Keep going. Do not stop. We are on your divine path together. You have nothing to fear. You are brave. I know you are brave and fearless as you should be. You will learn many tongues, all tongues in due time. Just let everything unfold as I tell you. Many will want to tell you what to do. You are to listen to me only. If you are not sure, just tell them I will need to pray on it and wait for the answer from the Lord.

They will understand. You are progressing and work is needed to be done. The pace will pick up again. You will see. Do not anticipate. Just let it unfold. I will protect you. Do not fear or be afraid about anything on earth or spiritually. You are protected. You deserve the good things of life and you will get them. As you serve your God, be strong, stay strong. Now go, my child, go in peace.

Yes, Jesus.

Week 6, Day 4: Tuesday, November 3, 2009

At 1:16 a.m. in the morning, I said, "Good morning, dear Jesus. Do you have anything to say?"

You are doing a good job. Keep up the good work. You will start back working soon. Get the book. You need to read up on spiritual warfare before Friday. You are obedient and you will. You are being talked about. Everyone wants to meet you and they will soon. Don't worry. You are going to be all right. You will be successful in both worlds. Go now. Go in peace.

Thank you, Jesus.

". . . There are in the end three things that last: faith, hope, and love, and the greatest of these is love" (1 Cor. 13:13).

Good morning, dear Jesus. Do you have anything to say?

Yes. You are progressing along. Keep up the good work. Things are going as planned. You have lots of work ahead of you. You can do it. People are beginning to know who you are. They are going to want to talk to you. You will be able to perform many miracles, sometimes right on the spot. Do not fear, for I am always with you. No one can harm you. You need to prepare. You need to read the book on spiritual warfare at the library. I will let you know when you pick up the right book to read. You will check it out of the library to read before Friday. You will bring it back on Friday. Lots of work will be done on Friday. You will check it back in on Friday before you go to the seminar. Go now. Go in peace.

Thank you, Jesus.

Week 6, Day 5: Wednesday, November 4, 2009

Oh, thank you Jesus for choosing me. I am honored to be a vessel for you to give light to the world's darkness.

Good morning, dear Jesus. Do you have anything to say?

Yes. You are progressing along very well. This morning you will have a lot to do. You will find the book today. You will have time to read it. Don't be afraid. Everything is going to work out fine. You will see. You are the chosen one. No evil can touch you. Evil fears you because it knows your power. Keep on track. Stay focused.

You will be rewarded for your good deeds. Stay kind and humble. Keep doing what you are doing. Your work will pick up very soon. Friday is another big day. You are right not to anticipate but just to let things unfold. You are being talked about. People can hardly wait to see you on Friday. You will be pleasantly surprised how much people admire you. They know that you are special. They are happy to be blessed to be around you. You don't realize how people view you. That is what makes you so humble. You treat people like they are in your family. You will be happy. You deserve to be happy. You come from a bloodline of spiritual people, from saints and holy people. Go now. Go in peace.

Dear Jesus, may I ask you a question?

Yes. You are obedient. You did what you were instructed to do. You have the right book for spiritual warfare. Read the parts that I direct you to. You are doing a great job. Your workload is picking up. So stay focused.

Dear Jesus, is there anything else you have to say?

Yes. You are truly a good person. Keep up the good work. Go now. Go in peace.

Thank you, Jesus.

Week 6, Day 6: Thursday, November 5, 2009

"The spiritual fruits of God's kingdom help safeguard you from negative and destructive influences" (Berardino, 30).

"Have no anxiety at all, but in everything, by prayer and petition, with thanksgiving, make your request known to God. Then the peace of God that surpasses all understanding will guard your hearts and minds in Christ Jesus" (Phil. 4:6, 7).

Dear Jesus, you give me peace and tranquility. I feel so happy to be in your presence with such a wonderful relationship. I love you very much.

Dear Jesus, do you have anything to say?

Yes. You are about to embark upon a major task tomorrow. You will drive out an evil spirit in front of the group and the priest. They are going to be amazed at what will take place. You are obedient and will do as I say. This person knows she has an evil spirit in her. She no longer desires for it to possess her. She is praying that I will deliver her from it and I will through you. You will know who she is. She is going to begin acting strange in front of the group. The priest will know right away what is going on. When he approaches her, you will approach her too. The priest will start praying over her. You will begin to speak in tongues. The priest will know right away what is taking place. He will let you complete the exorcism.

You will cast out the evil from her body. Right away she is going to thank you. You must say in front of the group for everyone to hear, "It is not I, but the Father above. I am only a vessel for Jesus Christ."

Do not be afraid. You are protected from all evil. Remember, evil is afraid of you because it knows your power. The priest is going to want to speak with you. He knows the power that I have given you. He is in awe of what is going to take place in the seminar and for him to be a witness. The word is going to spread. Go now. Go in peace.

Oh, dear Jesus, am I supposed to be sad? I feel as though I am losing a part of myself. The quietness of living a private life is what I feel I'm losing. I am crying because I know I am losing it so quickly. I will be obedient and I will do what you tell me to do. I feel as though I am mourning the loss of a certain kind of freedom that I will no longer have. But I also know that I will help save many souls. I know it is definitely worth giving up my freedom to do that. I love you, dear Jesus. I cherish our relationship. It is like no other that I have ever had. Thank you for choosing me. I will be obedient.

Oh, dear Jesus, I am crying again. Thank you so much for telling me ahead of time so I can properly mourn the loss of my freedom. I am humble to you. I love you. I thank you for loving me enough to choose me. Please forgive me for this sadness that has come over me. I am sad but happy at the same time. Thank you, Jesus. I love you. My relationship with you is enough for me. I know there is work to do and I am here for you. I will be obedient.

Oh, Jesus, we have such a special relationship. I thank you so much for it. I love you and I want you to know how humble and grateful I am to be in your presence. Oh, dear Jesus, oh dear Jesus, oh dear Jesus . . . I am so lucky, I am so humble. I am so elated to be here with you. The feeling is so overwhelming. I love you. I thank you. I give glory to you. Thank you, Jesus, for allowing me this honor. The honor to be in your presence I cannot describe in words. Thank you, thank you, thank you.

I am ready to be obedient and deal with the lady prayer group member who I will cast out the evil in her body.

Week 6, Day 7: Friday morning, November 6, 2009

Oh, dear Jesus, thank you for giving me an opportunity to live a holy life with you by my side assisting you with saving souls.

"As we participate in the very life of the Trinity of God, everything we need to live a holy life is made available to us" (Berardino, 31).

"His divine power has bestowed on us everything that makes for life and devotion, through the knowledge of him who called us by his own glory and power. Through these he has bestowed on us the precious and very great promises, so that through them you may come to share in the divine nature, after escaping from the corruption that is in the world because of evil desire " (2 Pet. 1:3–4).

"For this very reason, make every effort to supplement your faith with virtue, virtue with knowledge, knowledge with self-control with endurance, endurance with devotion, devotion with mutual affection, and mutual affection with love. If these are yours and increase in abundance, they will keep you from being idle or unfruitful in the knowledge of our Lord Jesus Christ" (2 Pet. 1:5–8).

Good morning, Jesus. Do you have anything to say?

Yes. You are rested. You are ready for the battle. Don't worry. We will win. You have the power to overcome any evil and they know that. You will do as I instruct you to tonight. This evil, that you will remove, is deep rooted and has been in her for a very long time. She has known this and has been entertained with it for a very long time. However, she has been attending the seminar and realizes that this is evil entertainment and no longer wants it as a part of her. She has been praying for forgiveness and to remove this evil spirit. She wants to be close to God and knows she cannot until she gets rid of the evil inside of her.

It will happen tonight. You will go to the seminar tonight as you usually do. Sit wherever you like, but do not sit on the first row. When the priest starts his presentation, she is going to start doing weird things. The priest will know right away what is happening. He will walk over to her immediately to start praying over her. When the priest starts walking toward her, you will walk with him over to her. You will immediately start talking and praying in tongues. I say "talking" because you will not be singing in tongues. You will be talking to pray the evil out of her.

You will know when you have completed the exorcism because you will tell her, 'It is gone. God has set you free.' Everyone, including the priest, will be in awe of the action that just took place. Remember to tell them, 'It is not I, but the Father above. Jesus Christ set you free.' Go now. Go in peace. God has spoken.

Yes, Jesus. I will obey. I am ready to do battle, for you are my Lord and my Savior. Thank you, Jesus, for giving me the honor to be a vessel to help save souls. Thank you, thank you, thank you.

***

In week six, Jesus continued giving me assignments.

Jesus told me I would meet the priest who wants to know who helped the church member to walk, but it did not happen. What I found out that Jesus prophecy to me did not always happen when He said it would. When Jesus would say soon, it could mean in a few days, weeks, months or even years. The time soon was relative not precise. Know it is on God's time. I learned in week six not to anticipate the prophecy but to let them unfold. Some of you may already have experienced time lines with the Lord.

This week I felt a very close relationship with Jesus. A part of me cried because I knew I would give up a part of my privacy to the public. At the same time, I was so happy to have such a special relationship with Him. Jesus encouraged me. He told me I was doing well. I would be rewarded for my good deeds. Jesus told me that I came from a bloodline of spiritual people, from saints and holy people. I was looking forward to week seven.

Chapter 7

Week 7: Spiritual Warfare

"Finally, draw your strength from the Lord and from his mighty power. Put on the armor of God so that you may be able to stand firm against the tactics of the devil"
(Ephesian 6:10–11)

At the seminar on Friday night, November 6, 2009, there was a guest speaker—a priest who spoke on spiritual warfare. He spoke on the Armor of God and of his challenges when he experienced a face-to-face encounter with the devil.

I had received instruction from Jesus that morning regarding casting out a demon in one of the prayer members. I waited for the priest to go up to the member to start praying over her, but it never happened. I waited afterwards, thinking that maybe it was going to happen after the priest's presentation, but it never happened. I talked to the priest briefly before he left and he asked if he could talk to me about some of my experiences. I told him that I would have to ask Jesus if He wanted me to talk to him. The priest gave me his e-mail address and told me to e-mail him after I talked to Jesus. On the way leaving, the priest said that I would e-mail him tonight and then again in the morning and that I would understand later.

When I went home that night, I wanted to pray and ask Jesus about what happened at the seminar that night. What was going on? She did not come. What went wrong? I did not cast out the demon in the lady. So, I asked Jesus:

Good evening, dear Jesus, may I ask you a question?

Yes. You did not see her this evening. She did not come tonight. She will come another time in which you will perform the exorcism. The priest is curious about your gifts. It is okay to talk to him. He wants to know the type of experiences you had and are having. You will not be working with him. You have a separate mission from his. You will run across each other's paths now and then but not on a regular basis.

You will need to prepare for the next assignment. You have work to do and it is coming up soon. Within a few days you will be working again. This time you will console someone who is in need of emotional help. She is very fragile, so you will have to be very careful in what you say to her. She tried to call you tonight, but you did not answer her call. Call her tomorrow in the morning. She will be very happy to hear from you. You can e-mail the priest and tell him you have spoken to me and that it will be all right to talk to him. Go now. Go in peace.

Thank you, Jesus.

I e-mailed the priest before I went to bed and told him I would be able to talk to him.

The next morning, Jesus woke me up and said it was urgent that he spoke to me. I quickly got up to listen to His words. Jesus told me I would have to move faster this morning because something needed fixing. I would need to do an exorcism this morning on the priest. I would need to call the priest and remove it before he took a trip. I was instructed to call as soon as I finished talking with Jesus.

Jesus told me I was to perform the exorcism over the phone when I called the priest. After the exorcism, I was to tell the priest that I would speak to him when he returned from his trip. I called the priest and I performed the exorcism as I was instructed by Jesus to do.

Now, I knew why the priest said that I would e-mail him that night and again in the morning. I e-mailed him after speaking with Jesus that evening and informed the priest that I could talk to him. The next morning, I had to e-mail him to get his phone number so I could call him to perform the exorcism. Even though I already knew that the priest had special gifts from Jesus too, I didn't at the time understand what he meant by the e-mails until after Jesus spoke to me the next morning.

Besides the exorcism and other assignments, this was a very special week for me. Jesus gave me my spiritual name as Dr. Jacki. He told me that it would be very fitting for all the work I would be doing. I do have a doctorate in education and my students at school call me

Dr. Scott. My family and friends call me Jacki. Jesus Christ calls me Dr. Jacki. So, my spiritual/religious name is Dr. Jacki.

I recall in the Bible when Jesus gave Abram the name Abraham (Gen. 17: 5), his wife, Sarai, the name Sarah (Gen. 17: 15), and Jacob the name Israel (Gen. 35:10).Oh. Thank you, Jesus, for my name you want to call me.

In this week, my assignments began to pick up. Faith was a big lesson for me. Besides receiving the assignment to cast out demons in several people (a lady in the prayer group and a priest), I was asked to go to the 8:00 a.m. mass to meet a person who was distraught. I was told not to worry about what to say, because I would know. Still another assignment, I was told at work a person was going to approach me to talk about her problems. I was going to lay my hands on her and help her with her depression.

I learned a big concept about prayers and faith from this assignment to speak to a person who was depressed from work. The person did not show up. I did not understand why what Jesus told me did not come true.

Jesus explained to me that people have a free will to make their own decisions and choices in life. People who usually change their minds do not have faith. They don't really believe what they are praying for is going to happen.

Now, I understood how, "It is done unto you as you believe," and why people say to start acting like you already have something before you get it. So, when you receive the answer to your prayers, you will not only be anticipating it, you will be ready for it. Some say luck is where preparation meets opportunity. So when God provides an opportunity for you, you will be prepared through your belief (faith) to receive it.

"Whatever you ask for in prayer with faith, you will receive" (Matt. 21:22).

I learned from the church greeter that when you do not have faith and you know it, you can pray to Jesus to give you faith and He will.

Oh my! God is good. All the time, God is good.

Here are my journal entries for week seven.

Week 7, Day 1: Saturday, November 7, 2009

It was 6:05 in the morning. Good morning, Jesus. You said it was urgent for me to get up so you can talk to me. I am awake and at your mercy. Do you have something to say?

Yes. You are going to have to move faster today. Something has come up and needs to be fixed. You are to call the priest this morning. He is in dire need of an exorcism on him. A demon has been bothering him for some time now and he wants it removed before he takes his trip. You are to call him as soon as I finish talking to you. Tell him I have spoken that you are going to pray in tongues over him this morning before he takes his trip. You will tell him when the demon is removed. Wish him a safe and enjoyable trip and that you will talk with him when he gets back. Go now. Go in peace. I have spoken.

Dear Jesus, may I ask you a question?

Yes. You have the phone number—look again.

Oh, dear Jesus, can you give it to me?

E-mail him right away and ask for his phone number.

Thank you, Jesus.

He is going to e-mail you. He already told you that he was going to receive an e-mail from you today and that later you will understand what he is saying. As soon as he gets up, he is going to check his e-mail and he is going to send his phone number. Be patient, my child. He will e-mail you.

Thank you, Jesus.

The priest will wake up around 7:00 a.m. He will look at his e-mail before he will do anything this morning. He is anticipating your e-mail as he told you last night. Be patient. Fix your coffee and wait.

Thank you, Jesus.

You can drink your coffee while you wait. Relax, for you have work to do this morning with the priest.

Thank you, Jesus.

You will not work with the priest, but you will talk to him from time to time. You both have different divine paths but are connected with the same goal in saving souls.

I received an e-mail from the priest containing his phone number. I thanked him in my reply and proceeded to call him around 7:30 a.m. I told him that Jesus wanted me to call him and pray in tongues over him. I then proceeded to speak in tongues. It was loud, forceful, and took a lot of energy. I told him, 'It is gone, it is gone. It is not I, but the Father above. Jesus Christ did it. Have a safe trip and I will talk to you when you return. Good-bye.' I paused a moment, didn't hear anything, and then I hung up the phone at 7:38 a.m.

Thank you, Jesus, for using me as a vessel to do God's work. I love you so much. I am so humble to your word. Thank you, thank you, thank you.

I called my prayer partner to share my experiences with her. She shared with me about a client who was sick and having problems.

Dear Jesus, may I ask you a question?

Yes. Your prayer partner is to pray for her (client) specific ailments right away. As we speak, she is in dire need of medical help. Your prayers and prayer partner will help her tremendously. Start praying right now. God has spoken.

Jesus spoke to me again.

Your spiritual name is Dr. Jacki. It is very fitting for all the spiritual work you are embarking upon.

Dear Jesus, may I ask you a question? (This question was referring to me regarding this morning in performing the exorcism to the priest over the phone.)

Yes. You did a great job this morning. Yes, he heard every word you said in prayer. He is elated with the exorcism that just happened with him. He can hardly wait to come back so he can sit down and talk to you. He knows that you are very powerful in the Word and that you are obedient.

Thank you, Jesus.

***

I am so thankful of God's Kingdom and share in the light which darkness cannot put out. I am ever so thankful for your powerful protection against evil for me.

"Strengthen with every power. In accord with his glorious might, for all endurance and patience, with joy giving thanks to the Father, who made you fit to share in the inheritance of the holy ones in light. He delivered us from the power of darkness and transferred us to the kingdom of his beloved son, in whom we have redemption, the forgiveness of sin" (Col. 1:11–14).

Thank you, Jesus, for allowing me to be a vessel to drive out a demon this morning. I am ever so humble in your presence.

Dear Jesus, do you have anything to say?

Yes. You are doing God's work well. You are being very obedient. You will be rewarded for it. There is still a lot of work to do. Keep up the good work. Go now. Go in peace and wait for day two.

Thank you, Jesus.

Week 7, Day 2: Sunday, November 8, 2009

Thank you, Jesus, for protecting me from evil and allowing me to be your vessel to get rid of evil from people. I am so grateful for all the gifts you have bestowed upon me.

"The strength of Jesus Christ which frees us from evil is stronger than all the combined forces of darkness" (Berardino, 36).

"Now since the children share in blood and flesh, he likewise shared in them, that through death he might destroy the one who has the power of death, that is, the devil, and free those who through fear of death had been subject to slavery all their life" (Heb. 2:14–15).

Good morning, dear Jesus. Do you have anything to say?

Yes. This is going to be a time of rest. You are doing a good job. People are talking. They want to meet you. They know that you have special powers and they want to talk to you about it. Don't worry. I will protect you. You are obedient and you will be rewarded for doing so. Soon you will start back to work, but you must rest now for the next task you will embark upon. Go now. Go in peace.

Thank you, Jesus.

***

Here are my thoughts throughout day one of week seven.

I saw the church greeter. She was sitting at the door of the church, greeting us as we went in. I saw her cane leaning against the wall near where she was sitting. After church, there were coffee and donuts. I bought two donuts and a cup of coffee. I sat at a table by myself. The church member approached me. Her cane was dangling on her arm as she carried a donut in one hand and a cup of coffee in the other.

As she approached me, I said, "You can walk."

She sat down next to me and said, "Oh, I can walk, but I need my cane because if I fall, my knee can shatter." I told her Jesus said she could walk. She said, "I can walk at home, but I use my cane when I go to church and when I am out of the house."

Two of her friends sat with us. The church greeter was going to the mall again, so I offered to drop her off. Just before she got out of the car, I told her, Jesus said, "He has healed you. You can walk without your cane."

She said, "I know Jesus is trying to convince me. I will keep praying," and she walked away, using her cane as if she could not walk without it.

It is done unto you as you believe. The church member could walk but she did not have faith. To say Jesus is trying to convince her means she doesn't believe in Jesus. If she did, she would know she could because Jesus told her so.

The Healing of Two Blind Men: "And as Jesus passed on from there, two blind men followed [him], crying out 'Son of David, have pity on us!' when he entered the house, the blind men approach him and Jesus said o them, 'Do you believe that I can do this?' Yes Lord, they said to him. Then he touched their eyes and said, 'Let it be done for you according to your faith.' And their eyes were opened. Jesus warned them sternly 'See that no one knows about this'" (Matt. 9:27–30).

"Whatever you ask for in prayer with faith, you will receive" (Matt. 21:22).

Good evening, dear Jesus. May I ask you a question? I wanted to know if the church greeter could walk without her cane.

Yes. You are doing a good job. The church member can now walk and she now knows she can walk without her cane. She is elated that you were right. I did heal her. She can walk without the need of her cane. She has told the priest what has happened, and she told him that you told her that I, Jesus, healed her. The priest is going to call you this week. Yes, she is now a believer. She knows she can walk. Go now. Go in peace.

Thank you, Jesus.

Week 7, Day 3: Monday, November 9, 2009

Dear Jesus, I place myself under full submission to God. I do not fear the devil, for he doesn't have any influence over me.

"Therefore submit to God: resist the devil and he will take flight" (James 4:7).

Good morning, dear Jesus. Do you have anything to say?

Yes, you are on the right path. Everything is going as planned. You will begin work again. Do not be afraid. I am always with you. No evil can embark upon you. You are strong in the Word. You are a soldier of God. We are going to bring about many happy souls. They are going to be so very grateful for the work we will do together.

You are ready now to begin our journey. You will do many things. Not just casting out evil, but you will perform miracles like no one has ever seen in this lifetime. You are submissive to God. You truly do not fear evil. You know the power of Jesus. You know I will protect you.

Remember, you take direction from me. Many are going to want to join forces with you to take the glory of your work. I will not allow it, for you will be very clear that it is Jesus Christ that has done the work, not you. I already know that you will be obedient.

The time is near to begin working again. You will begin by going to the eight o'clock mass this morning. You will meet a person who is distraught. She will come up to you explaining how she feels. You will lay hands on that person to feel better. Do not worry about what to say. The right words will come at the right time. I have spoken. Go now. Go in peace.

Thank you, Jesus.

***

I went to the 8:00 mass this morning. When I left after mass, I walked slowly to give anyone wanting to approach me an opportunity to do so. I went to my car and I just stood outside waiting to see if anyone was going to come up to me. No one did. So I asked Jesus if I could I ask Him a question.

Yes. The person did not come to church this morning. You can go. I have spoken.

So I left. Thank you, Jesus, for giving me this opportunity to do God's work.

Dear Jesus, do you have anything to say?

Yes. You are obedient. You did what I asked you to do. The person is so distraught that she could not even get up to go to mass this morning. So, you will pray for her this morning in tongues. After you finish, she will feel much better. Go now. I have spoken.

Thank you, Jesus.

Dear Jesus, I have prayed in tongues for this person that is in need. Do you have anything to say?

Yes. You are obedient. She is feeling better as we speak. You are progressing quite well now. You are to receive more gifts on Friday at the seminar. A priest is going to return. He will return to the seminar to complete the presentation on the spiritual gifts. It is then that you will be given the gift to interpret tongues. You will interpret the priest when he speaks in tongues. He will know because he can interpret his own tongues but not others. You will be able to interpret all tongues. Go now. Go in peace.

Thank you, Jesus.

Week 7, Day 4: Tuesday, November 10, 2009

I wear the armor of God to resist the evil throughout the day. Evil cannot do anything to me. I am protected by Jesus Christ. Thank you, Jesus, for your protection against evil.

Battle against evil. "Finally, draw your strength from the Lord and from his mighty power. Put on the armor of God so that you may be able to stand firm against the tactics of the devil: For our struggle is not with flesh and blood but with principalities, with the powers with the world rulers of the present darkness, and with the evil spirits in the heavens" (Eph. 6:10–12).

"Therefore, put on the armor of God; that you may be able to resist on the evil day and, having done everything, to hold your ground. So stand fast with your loins girded in truth, clothed with righteousness as a breastplate, and your feet shod in readiness for the gospel of peace. In all circumstances hold faith as a shield, to quench all [the] flaming arrows of the evil one. And take the helmet of salvation and the sword of the spirit, which is the word of God" (Eph. 6:13–17).

Constant prayer: "With all prayer and supplication, pray at every opportunity in the Spirit. To that end, be watchful with all perseverance and supplication for all the holy ones" (Eph. 6:18).

Good morning, dear Jesus. Do you have anything to say?

Yes. Keep going. You are doing a great job. You are obedient. Stay the course. We are doing it according to plan. Do not worry about anything. You will be rewarded. You will be financially secured soon, neither worries nor bills. We have lots to do. You will not have time to worry about finances, classes, or anything of that nature. You are financially secure. Have faith.

The church member is a good example of not having faith in the beginning. One thing she did do was that she prayed to me to give her the faith that she needed and she received it. There are many lessons for you to learn how people think. Remember, everyone cannot think the same as you. They will not have the vision or foresight that you have. So, stay the course, and keep obeying as I know you will.

Now it is time for more work. You will help a person today who is deeply depressed. No one really knows that she is so depressed because she puts on her happy face for work but she is really hurting inside. She has prayed to me to help her with her depression. You will go to work today as usual. She is going to approach you with her problems. For some reason, she is going to feel that she can talk to you and she is right. You are going to tell her that Jesus told you that she was going to come to you today and that I have spoken.

You are to lay your hands on her to get rid of her depression. She is going to be very receptive. You will do it in your office. Immediately after you do it, she is going to have a heavy burden lifted from her. Go now. I have spoken. Go in peace.

Thank you, Jesus.

***

Here are my thoughts throughout day four of week seven.

No one approached me with their problems today at work. It was now in the afternoon and I have been here since 7:15 a.m.

Good afternoon, dear Jesus. May I ask you a question?

Yes. You are obedient. The person is not there. She did not want to talk today. She will eventually get around to talking to you but not today. You may leave if you like. Go now. Go in peace.

Dear Jesus, may I ask you another question?

Yes. They have a free will and can make changes at will. They often change their mind when they do not have faith. They really do not believe what they are praying for is going to really happen. You are obedient. You did what you were supposed to do. Go now. Go in peace.

Thank you, Jesus.

Week 7, Day 5: Wednesday, November 11, 2009

Dear Jesus, I yield to your divine power, which overcomes the spiritual strongholds of darkness.

"For a while your obedience is known by all, so that I rejoice over you, I want you to be wise as to what is good, and simple as to what is evil; then the God of peace will quickly crush Satan under your feet. Thy grace of our Lord Jesus be with you" (Rom. 16:19, 20).

Good morning, dear Jesus. Do you have anything to say?

Yes. You are moving in the right direction. Keep going. You are doing great. The time has come to continue working. Now you will go to church this morning and the priest is going to approach you. He now knows that you performed the miracle for a church member. You are to tell him that it is not I, but the Father above. It must be very clear that I, Jesus Christ, performed the miracle. I have spoken. Go now. Go in peace.

Thank you, Jesus.

***

I went to the 8:00 a.m. Wednesday morning mass as directed. During the mass, an elderly parishioner fell and the paramedics were called to take him to the hospital. Mass continued, and the priest went over and gave those who had assisted the elderly parishioner Holy Communion. After the mass, the priest went over to the elderly parishioner to see what he could do. The priest looked over at me. I asked Jesus if I could ask him a question. He said yes and told me to stay afterwards to say the rosary with the group who stayed after mass to pray. He told me that the priest saw me. So I stayed and finished the rosary. I left the church, but the priest was not around. I went to my car and asked Jesus if I could ask him a question. He said yes and He told me I could leave now.

Good morning, dear Jesus. May I ask you a question?

Yes. You were obedient. The priest was distracted this morning, but he was very aware that you were at church this morning. He is going to call you this week. He is anxious to hear what you have to say. Go now. Go in Peace.

Thank you, Jesus.

Week 7, Day 6: Thursday, November 12, 2009

Thank you, Jesus, for giving me the freedom from the evil forces.

"We must never forget that the freedom we have from the forces of evil is not due to any of our efforts but comes totally through the grace of God" (Berardino, 38).

> You were dead in your transgressions and sins in which you once lived following the age of this world, following the ruler of the power of the air, the spirit that is now at work in the disobedient. All of us once lived among them in the desires of our flesh, following the wishes of the fresh and the impulses, and we were by nature children of wrath, like the rest. But God, who is rich in mercy, because of the great love he had for us, even when we were dead in our transgressions, brought

us to life with Christ (by grace you have been saved) (Eph. 2:1–5).

Good morning, dear Jesus. Do you have anything to say?

Yes. You are progressing quite well. You are obedient. Your work is continuing. Today you will need to drive out the devil in someone at work. She is being tormented by this evil spirit. She will come to you in desperate need of help. She will know you can drive out the evil spirit in her. You will tell her that Jesus is going to drive out the evil spirit. You will speak tongues over her. You will tell her when it is gone. Make sure you tell her that I, Jesus, drove out the evil spirit. You will do it in your office this morning before you start your classes. I have spoken. Go now. Go in peace.

Thank you, Jesus.

***

Here are my thoughts for day six of week seven.

This morning I went to work, but no one approached me. After asking you the question, you mentioned that it was one of my students, but he did not come to school today. You said it would happen another day.

Dear Jesus, may I ask you a question?

Yes. The student did not come today. He is having a hard time with these demons and it is time for them to go. They must go now. When I finish talking to you, you will speak in tongues to get rid of the demons in him. On Tuesday, you will tell him that I have spoken, and that on Thursday, at 4:30 p.m., I got rid of the demons for him. He can now stay focused and do what he needs to do. Go now. I have spoken.

Thank you, Jesus.

Dear Jesus, I (as your vessel for you) have cast out the demons in the student. He is no longer afraid of tall buildings because you have gotten rid of his fears. He started believing in you again, and prayed for you to help him and you did. Thank you, Jesus, for choosing me as your vessel to do so. Thank you, thank you, thank you.

Week 7, Day 7: Friday morning, November 13, 2009

I thank you, Jesus, for designating me to be thy servant. I am honored for you to send me to turn people from darkness to the light and from the dominion of Satan to God. I love you, dear Jesus.

> Get up now and stand on your feet. I have appeared to you for this purpose, to appoint you as a servant and witness of what you have seen [of me] and what you will be shown. I shall deliver you from this people and from the gentiles to whom I send you, to open their eyes that they may turn from darkness to light and from the power of Satan to God, so that they may obtain forgiveness of sins an inheritance among those who have been consecrated by faith in me (Acts 26: 16–18).

Good morning, dear Jesus. Do you have anything to say?

Yes. This is the day. You have lots of work to do. You will go to the seminar tonight and you will learn how to interpret tongues, all tongues. The people there will be amazed to be a witness. The priest will know because the priest can interpret his own tongues, but he cannot interpret all tongues.

You will also cast out the devil in a person who did not come last week but whom will be there tonight. She is going to do some strange things. The priest will know and he is going to walk toward her to begin praying over her. You will walk with him, and you will begin speaking tongues. Either way is fine. You will tell her when it is gone. Make sure that you tell her and everyone that it is not you but the Father above. You are only a channel for Jesus. Jesus Christ cast out the devil in her.

You will get there early. You will sit anywhere but in the first row. No one will have a clue of what they are about to witness tonight because you are going to cast out more than one devil tonight. You will know whom because he or she will start acting strange, and again the priest will walk over to them to start praying over them. You will speak in tongues again. You will tell him when the devil is gone.

Again, make sure that you tell them that, "It is not I but the Father above. Jesus Christ cast out the devil." You will cast out the devil from three people in total, but not all at the same time. They will be at different times. The priest is also prepared to do what he is supposed to do. He does not know that it is you. He will be somewhat surprised, but he will remember that you received the gift of tongues. I know this is a lot for you to take in today. Don't worry; you will have the strength to cast out evil. I will give you all the strength you need. You are obedient and I know you will obey. After tonight, your name is going to begin to resonate among the parishes. They will know a beautiful woman is powerful in the Word and they will all want to meet you. Have faith, stand strong, for you are about to embark upon your spiritual journey like never before. I have spoken. Go now. Go in peace.

Thank you, Jesus.

***

Chapter seven deals with spiritual warfare. I had several assignments regarding the casting out of evil. He told me I would cast out a demon in a prayer group member in front of the prayer group and the priest, but it did not happen. I asked Jesus about it and He told me the lady did not come. It would happen later and it did. I was given another assignment to drive out the devil in someone at work. It did not happen this week but it did eventually happen. Jesus had me to speak in tongues at home at 4:30 p.m. to drive out the devil in the Veteran student. It happened and the student remembered the time it happened for him.

Jesus told me I would not just be given assignments for casting out evil but I will perform miracles. I was given other assignments such as I would council someone who had need in emotional help. I had to attend an 8:00 a.m. mass to counsel, but the person did not attend mass that morning. During week seven, I asked the church greeter if she could walk without her cane. She said yes. She could walk at home and she uses the cane when she goes to church.

Jesus also explained to me that people have a free will to make their own decisions. We make decision to accept the gifts Jesus gives us and to use them as God intends for us to use them. Our special gifts are irrevocable. Chapter eight speaks to the gifts of the spirit.

Chapter 8

Week 8: The Gifts of the Spirit

"There are different kinds of spiritual gifts but with the same Spirit" (1 Corinthians 12:4)

At the seminar on Friday night, November 13, 2009, the topic was on the gifts of the spirit. That night I was supposed to cast out demons in three members. I was disappointed when it didn't take place. When I returned home, I asked Jesus if I could ask him a question.

Dear Jesus, may I ask you a question?

Yes. You were obedient. You did what you were supposed to do. Tonight was not the night. All three were there, but they are not ready for the demon to be removed. You will cast out demons in them later. You did nothing wrong. You were obedient and that is what matters.

Do not worry about how things turn out. That is not your concern. Your concern is to obey. And you did. God will reward you for it. Keep moving in the right direction. People are already talking about you and they will continue. They know that you have special gifts. They are just curious of how many you have. You will interpret tongues soon. Go now. Go in peace.

Thank you, Jesus.

From the Friday night seminar, Jesus taught me that I was to be obedient and do as I was told. I was not to worry about the outcome. The outcome was not my concern.

In this eighth week of the seminar, I was thankful for the gifts given to me—thank you, Jesus. I thank you for the gifts of faith, messages, discernment, wisdom, knowledge, casting out evil, healing, counseling, speaking in tongues, interpretation of tongues, and prophecy. I was ever so grateful for so many. However, I was fully aware of the responsibility that came with these gifts.

". . . everyone to whom much is given, from him much will be required . . ." (Luke 12:48).

One night during week eight, I had something to ask Jesus and instead of asking, "May I ask a question?" I asked Him if He had something to say. Jesus said, "No." I felt rejected by Jesus for the first time. I was devastated.

I really had a question to ask, and I should have asked the question rather than asking if Jesus had something to say. I now knew that I needed to ask the question.

Jesus told me He would tell me whatever I needed to know. He also told me that when He gave you a spiritual gift, it was forever. The spiritual gift was irrevocable. There was no turning back.

I received another experience from Jesus about how things did not go exactly as planned because of free will. People were not always obedient nor did they believe or have faith. When I received an assignment in the morning and would go on my merry way to complete the assignment, the assignments did not take place as I was told they would.

One morning, I was given the assignment to counsel a student who was depressed. The student would come up to me. Well, it never happened that day. I wondered why. Later, Jesus told me that the student did not come to school that day. I did eventually see the student, and Jesus was able to counsel the student through me.

I also asked Jesus to teach me more about faith. He taught it to me this week with my eye. Jesus told me this experience would be my signature example of faith.

One morning, as I was getting ready for work, it felt like something was in my eye. It felt like an eyelash or a grain of salt or sand. As I was trying to get it out, a thought came to me from Jesus—*have faith and it will go away*. He repeated it—*have faith and it will go away*. I kept saying, "Thank you, Jesus, for clearing my eye." I said this all the way to work. It wasn't until I got to work that it went away. So it wasn't until then that my belief system believed it was gone.

There was another lesson I learned about faith. When Jesus answers our prayers, we have to believe that He actually did it. When I delivered messages, some who received the messages did not believe or realize that their prayers were answered. I wondered how they could not believe. Jesus said to have patience with those who did not believe or have faith. He taught me a lesson through my own personal experience.

One morning I woke up with a sinus headache. I was also instructed that morning to go to the 8:00 a.m. mass. Jesus told me that morning not to worry, because my sinus headache would go away. Well, I went to mass and my sinus headache wasn't as bad as when I woke up, but it still did not go away completely.

So, there I was in mass and the headache began to get worse. I questioned whether I should take some medication or believe in what Jesus told me. *The headache will go away.* I started praying about it in mass. *Please, Jesus, make this headache go away.* Jesus said to me, "You must have faith." Right away, I knew the lesson Jesus was teaching me. I thanked Jesus for getting rid of my headache. Faith is not easy to receive; that is why it is said that if you have the pure faith as small as a mustard seed, you will be able to move mountains (Matt. 17:20–21). I no longer criticize those who have a hard time believing and having faith in Jesus. I myself, am still working at having "pure" faith as small as a mustard seed.

The following are my journal entries for week eight of the seminar.

Week 8, Day 1: Saturday, November 14, 2009

I thank you for the gifts that you have bestowed upon me. I know you gave me the gift of prophecy, speaking in tongues, interpretation of tongues, wisdom, knowledge, discernment, miracles, faith, healing, counseling, and teaching. I believe you have given me these gifts. Thank you, thank you, thank you.

Good morning, dear Jesus. Do you have anything to say?

Yes. You are obedient. You are doing what you are supposed to do. You will be rewarded for it. Now we must continue our work. Today you will go to the movies with your colleague. She is very depressed. She has a lot of pride, so she is masking it. You will be of great comfort for her. You will tell her that she is not to worry about anything. God has spoken. Go now. Go in peace.

Dear Jesus, may I ask a question?

Yes. You will tell her God has spoken. She will know exactly what you are talking about because she is also powerful in the Word and has been for years. Do not tell her not to worry until she has told you her problems, thoughts, and fears. She trusts you and cherishes your friendship. She has missed talking to you from time to time. She is excited to go to the movies with you. She doesn't have many friends. Most of her friends have passed away, crossed over to the other side. You will have a good time today, and you will feel good afterwards because you will know that you helped her. Go now. Go in peace. I have spoken.

Thank you, Jesus.

Dear Jesus, may I ask you another question?

Yes. I have given you many gifts already, but I still have more to give you. You will receive all the gifts because you have been chosen to do many things. You are obedient, and I must have someone who is obedient, sincere, kind, loving, humble, and true to me. You are all of these and more. You will be rewarded for your obedience. I know you were a little disappointed last night, but you stayed true to me, and you will be rewarded.

I mentioned to you before how sometimes things do not go exactly as planned because you have a free will. Everyone is not as obedient as you are, nor do they believe and have faith. Everyone doesn't see things the way you do. You have the gift of discernment. Many do not have this gift. You have the gift of wisdom. I can tell you to do something and I know it will be done. You already have many gifts, for you have already used them. You have more gifts of the spirit to come. Have patience. Stay true to the Word. You have a lot of work ahead of you. You will be rewarded. You will be able to do it all, for I have spoken. Go now. Go in peace.

Thank you, Jesus.

Week 8, Day 2: Sunday, November 15, 2009

I will never take for granted the seriousness of the redemption Jesus Christ has wrought for us.

Therefore, we must attend all the more to what we have heard, so that we may not be carried away. Or if the Word announced through angels proved firm, an every transgression and disobedience received its just recompense, how shall we escape if we ignore so great a salvation? Announced originally through the Lord, it was confirmed for us by those who had heard. God added his testimony by signs, wonders, various acts of power, and the distribution of gifts of the Holy Spirit according to his will" (Heb. 2:1–4).

Good morning, dear Jesus. Do you have anything to say?

Yes. You are doing well. Everything is going as planned. Keep up the good work. We must begin again doing our work in saving souls. Today you will go to church and you will be surprised at the number of people who are going to want to talk to you. Yes, they know about the miracle with the church member. The priest is back, and he is going to want to talk to you too. You must remind people who is performing the miracle. You must say, 'It is not I, but the Father above. Jesus Christ is performing the miracles.' Everything is going as planned. After church today, you will go home and rest. You have a big week ahead of you. Go now. I have spoken. Go in peace.

Don't worry. Everything is all right. You did a good job with your colleague. Your colleague is very pleased to hear her message from me. Remember, Dr. Jacki, you must have faith. You must believe you are doing a good job doing God's work. I do not always have to tell you that you are. I know it was the first time last night that I said, "No, I do not have anything to say." Do not take it as rejection. I will tell you what you need to know when the time presents itself. Even though I do not have anything to say, I am still with you. I still love you and will always protect you. You are chosen. It can never be revoked. You are safe. Go now. Go in peace.

Thank you, Jesus.

Dear Jesus, may I ask you a question? I was beginning to feel tired from the energy expended from the spiritual work I was doing.

Yes. Yes, you may do whatever you like. You are resting from helping souls today. I realize that it takes energy to save souls, and I will allow down time so that you are properly rested. Go now. Go in peace.

Thank you, Jesus. I thank you for all the gifts and things you have done for me.

Week 8, Day 3: Monday, November 16, 2009

I know all gifts from God are good and that I will always properly use them by the instructions of God, Jesus Christ. I will always be obedient. Thank you, Jesus, for my gifts you have bestowed upon me. Thank you, thank you, thank you.

Good morning, dear Jesus. Do you have anything to say?

Yes. It is time to go back to work. You will go to church this morning. You will see the priest this morning. He wants to talk to you. You will spend a little time with him after mass. He is excited to talk to you. He wants to thank you for being obedient and driving out the demon in him. He has had it for a long time, and he is so relieved to have it removed. Go now. I have spoken. Go in peace.

Dear Jesus, may I ask you a question?

Yes. You have a sinus headache this morning, but it will not last long. You will not have your headache after mass when you are talking to the priest. Go now. Go in peace.

Thank you, Jesus.

***

I went to the eight o'clock mass. Jesus told me that my sinus headache would go away and I would not have it after church. In church, however, I still had the headache. I was praying about it. Jesus spoke to me and said I had to have faith. I now understood how people could doubt their faith when they were sick. He gave an example of the church member who could now walk without her cane but didn't have faith to believe that she could. I knew my headache would go away because Jesus had already told me that it would go away. Right then I should have forgotten about it and just let Jesus take care of it. Instead, I began to pray to Jesus to help me to have faith even after Jesus said it would go away. I had to be humble and understand people who were healing. Sometimes they did not see it even when they were healed. In church, I said, "Oh, Jesus, I get it. I am sorry that I had to experience before I understood."

I left church and went to my car. I did not see the priest. I sat in the car and Jesus told me I could go.

On the way home, I began to feel very bad. I started to cry because I didn't have the faith that I thought I did. I cried because I knew I had let Jesus down, that I was fooling myself thinking that I had faith in Him. It was almost like conditional faith. I believed Jesus when things were going well or as planned but then somewhat questioned Him when it didn't. I was still praying for faith.

Oh, dear Jesus, please give me the gift of faith. Make me so humble and pure in your love. I sincerely feel bad that I let you down. I love you so much. We have such a special relationship that I never want to lose. I know this morning I was feeling bad with a terrible sinus headache, and that I didn't have the desire to be obedient and actually want to go to church, but I did.

Please forgive me. I want to be a good soldier for you, Jesus Christ. Please give me the gift of faith. Teach me how to be faithful to you. Teach me how to understand those who have received miracles and do not have the faith to know it. Teach me how to be humble in the faith of you, Jesus. I want our relationship to grow closer and closer each day. Please forgive me. I love you so very much. I am even ashamed to have cried because I will have to give up some of my privacy to save souls. Saving souls is so important. I am here for you, Jesus. I am your soldier. I am here at your mercy. May I please have the gift of faith? I love you, Jesus. Please forgive me.

Dear Jesus, may I ask you questions?

Yes. You are forgiven. I love you too. We do have a special relationship. There many lessons for you to learn, and this is only one of them. You need not spend any more time mourning over this lesson. We have plenty of work ahead of us to do. A lesson well learned. It is done unto you as you believe is in the Bible. Take heed of these words.

They are so powerful. As you can see and feel, your headache has gone away. Now you do believe and I give you the gift of faith. You will have faith like you have never had before. Go now. I am with you always. Go in peace. I have spoken.

It is done unto you as you believe. My prayer partner will find it in the Bible—Matt. 8:13, Matt. 21:21, Luke 17:5, Luke 1:38, Luke 10:23, and Luke 11:28.

Week 8, Day 4: Tuesday, November 17, 2009

Our dear Jesus has distributed the spiritual gifts among us. I thank you Jesus for the spiritual gifts that you have bestowed upon me.

". . . All good giving and every perfect gift is from above, coming down from the Father of lights, with whom there is no alteration of shadow caused by change" (James 1:17).

Good morning, dear Jesus. Do you have anything to say?

Yes. Everything is going as planned. You are doing a great job. You will need to continue working. Today you will talk to your student. You will tell him that last Thursday at 4:30 p.m., I, Jesus, drove out the demons in him. He will know exactly what you are talking about. He no longer fears tall buildings. He will mention to you that he knew it was Jesus and that I had something to do with it. Tell him Jesus Christ drove out the evil in him. Say to him, "It is not I, but the Father above." Go now. I have spoken. Go in peace.

Thank you, Jesus.

***

I gave the message to a student as Jesus told me to. I said, "Jesus told me to tell you that last week on Thursday, November 12, 2009, at 4:30 p.m., Jesus drove out a demon in you and you no longer have fear of tall buildings."

This morning at school, Jesus told me to also tell him, "Whenever fear comes, say, 'Jesus said my fear is gone.'"

I felt good about the student. He wasn't all fidgety and slightly irritated the way he usually was. I told Jesus that before class and after class, the student said he is going to meditate on what I told him. He said he was really upset on Veterans Day.

When Jesus told me to tell the student to say, "Jesus said, my fear is gone," it reminded me of thanking Jesus for clearing my eye over and over until it cleared. I knew it did not clear until I fully believed that Jesus cleared it.

Week 8, Day 5: Wednesday, November 18, 2009

I am thankful for the gifts given to me—thank you, Jesus. I thank you for the gifts of faith, performing miracles, delivering messages, discernment, wisdom, knowledge, casting out evil, healing, counseling, speaking in tongues, interpreting tongues, and prophecy.

"The Spirit of the Lord shall rest upon him; The Spirit of Wisdom and understanding, The Spirit of Counsel and Might, The Spirit Knowledge and the fear of the Lord" (Is. 11:2).

Good morning, dear Jesus. Do you have anything to say?

Yes. You did a good job yesterday. I am pleased with the student's outcome. He understands the meaning of 4:30 p.m. He is also coming along his divine path. The time is coming near to do more work. You will go to school today and see one of your students having a hard time. She is feeling terrible inside. She is extremely depressed. You will comfort her to the point that she will no longer want to commit suicide. You will know who she is because she is going to ask to speak to you in private. She is desperate to talk to someone. Wait for more instructions later on today.

You will know when I am talking to you. You are obedient. You and your prayer partner will make excellent healing partners. Yes, healing partners. You both will have the gift of healing soon. You are doing a good job. You are learning the gift of faith. You did a good job with the healing of your eye. Yes, you heard me when I said have faith and it will go away. You did the right thing for thanking me for clearing the stuff in your eye. You now know the power of healing and the power of faith. You have more gifts to receive, and you will receive them soon. Go now. Go in peace. I have spoken.

Dear Jesus, may I ask you a question? (I was curious about the difference between a pastor and a minister.)

Yes. The difference is the way they preach their sermons. Pastors reside over the church. Ministers who are called reverend preach in the church but are not over the church. Go now. Go in peace.

Thank you, Jesus.

Dear Jesus, may I ask you another question? (I was wondering if I should let people know I can talk to Him (Jesus) directly any time I want.)

Yes. You, by all means, let him know that you have a direct line to Jesus Christ. In time, the world will know. Go now. Go in peace. I have spoken.

Thank you, Jesus.

***

On Wednesday, November 18, 2009, the student approached me in class during the lab time prior to the online practical exam. She looked discourage and wasn't very talkative. I told her that I talked to Jesus this morning and He told me that one of my students was going to come to me depressed.

I talked to her for several minutes to encourage her. She said that she was homeless and felt like no one even cared about her. We talked and then Jesus starting talking to me. He told me to tell her that she could go to a shelter. I told her. We continued talking, and then I stopped because Jesus starting talking to me again. He told me to tell her that someone was going to take a liking to her and was going to help her at the next shelter she went to.

I talked about how lucky she was to have intelligence and good looks. She had a lot to be thankful for. She needed to turn to Jesus to help her instead of all those other people who were not helping. She felt alone, but I told her she was never alone. She always had Jesus. I made it clear to her that Jesus sought her out to let her know that she was loved and He did not want her to commit suicide. I really got her attention, because she knew what I said was the truth. She felt like committing suicide.

She took the test and afterwards she told me she only missed one question. I knew she was waiting for me to say how well she did and so I told her. She smiled and was proud of herself. As she walked out of the classroom, I told her to wait a minute. We were both standing in the hallway when I asked if she needed a hug. She smiled and I hugged her.

I really felt good afterwards because I really like helping people. Thank you, Jesus, for using me to help my student.

Week 8, Day 6: Thursday, November 19, 2009

I am so lucky that the message of Jesus has become so firmly planted in me that I lack no spiritual gift that I am in need of.

"For what man knows the things of a man except the spirit of the man which is in him? Even so no one knows the things of God except the Spirit of God" (1 Cor. 2: 10).

> Among human beings, who knows what pertains to a person except the spirit of the person that is within? Similarly, no one knows what pertains to God except the Spirit of God. We have not received the spirit of the world but the spirit that is from God, so that we may understand the things freely given us by God. And we speak about them not with words taught by human wisdom, but with words taught by the Spirit, describing spiritual realities in spiritual terms" (1 Cor. 2:11–13).

"Now the natural person does not accept what pertains to the Spirit of God, for to him it is foolishness, and he cannot understand it, because it is judged spiritually" (1 Cor. 2:14).

Good morning, Jesus. Do you have anything to say?

Yes. You are coming along just fine. You have more work to do. You will see the person who didn't come up to you at school who needed to have a demon removed. She is extremely uncomfortable and will ask for your help. For some reason, she is aware of your gifts through someone else. She will approach you this morning. She will ask you to come into her office to talk for a few minutes. You will go. As soon a she asks you to go to her office, you will know that she is the one. You will speak in tongues and remove the demon from her. When it leaves, you will say it is gone. Remember, you must tell her, 'It is not I, but the Father above. Jesus Christ removed the demon.' Go in Peace. I have spoken.

Thank you, Jesus.

Dear Jesus, may I ask you another question? I am through school and nothing happened today.

Yes. Today was not the day. She did not choose to ask you for some reason. She may be hesitating, but she will get around to asking you. She called you into her office, but she got cold feet. She played it off with the e-mail problem. As soon as she called you into the office, you knew it was she, and you were right. She will ask you soon. Don't worry; you will have plenty of work to do at the seminar. You will know tomorrow. I have already discussed it with you earlier this week. Go now. Go in peace.

Thank you, Jesus.

Week 8, Day 7: Friday morning, November 20, 2009

I am so blessed to know that "We are to always exercise discernment because some things may have the appearance of a spiritual gift but not be authentic" (Berardino, 35).

Good morning, dear Jesus. Do you have anything to say?

Yes. Time has come to do real work today. You will go early to the seminar tonight. You will sit in the front row. You will learn how to speak in tongues and at the same time interpret them. When the priest speaks in tongues, you will know what he is saying. As he speaks before everyone in tongues, you will begin to interpret it. He will know that you can interpret because he can only interpret his own tongues. You will be able to interpret all tongues.

You have other work to do. Tonight you will be able to cast out the demons in the three people who did not come last week. They will be there tonight. So will the priest. He is anxious to talk to you. It will be the priest that will walk over to the person who begins to act weird. You will follow him over. The priest will begin praying, and you will begin to talk in tongues. You will tell this person when the demon is gone.

Make sure that you tell them that, "It is not I, but the Father above. Jesus Christ cast out the demon, not you." You and the priest will cast out the demons three times. Not all at once, but one after the other. For right when you finish with one and tell them that Jesus Christ did it, another person will start acting weird. You and the priest will cast out the demons until you have cast out all three. The priest knows his part in casting out the demons. He now knows you will do it with him. The people there who will witness this will fall to their knees. They will start praying, crying in awe in what they have just witnessed. Word is going to spread among the parishes. The pastor is going to want to talk to you right away. He wants to talk to you before others do.

Remember to tell them that Jesus Christ drove out the demons, not you. I know you will obey because you are an obedient servant like no other that I have ever seen in this lifetime. That is why I have chosen you. The priest was in awe of how you waited until he left before you went home. He knew then that you were very special and that he would be doing some work with you. You will do only some work together, for both of you has different divine paths. You will see each other from time to time to work together but will not work together on a regular basis. You will work with your prayer partner. You and your prayer partner have work to do together. Your divine paths are closer together but are not the same. You will work with your prayer partner, and you will work by yourself. You will also work with other people from time to time. For you will be worldwide in working with people and saving souls. Go now. I have spoken. Go in peace.

Dear Jesus, may I ask you a question? (I had a vision of me and my prayer partner at a children's hospital going around and healing children.)

Yes. You are right. You and your prayer partner will be healing children in a hospital but it is not soon. In due time, it will happen. Now go in peace.

Thank you, Jesus.

I went to church that night, but the priest who was supposed to attend the seminar did not attend.

Dear Jesus, may I ask you a question? I wasn't sure if I understood Jesus. I didn't see the priest.

Yes. You did the right thing. You were obedient. For some reason, the priest was not up to working tonight. He did not do what he was supposed to do. He was somewhat depressed tonight. He didn't even want to talk to you as he wanted to before. Everyone is not as obedient as you. That is why I chose you. You are obedient and consistent in doing so. Another time will present itself for you to do the exorcism. Don't worry. You have a lot of work ahead of you. We will talk tomorrow or this morning. Everything that you are doing is working as planned. Go now.

Thank you, Jesus.

***

In week eight, Jesus gave me the assignment to cast out evil in three of the seminar participants but it did not happen. Jesus said they were not ready yet. It would happen later and it did three months later after the seminar was over. After the seminar was over, the parish continued their charismatic prayer meetings at the same time on Friday evenings. It was in the prayer meeting in February 2010 that the three exorcisms took place in the same meeting. Since the seminar, I have also been a vessel for Jesus for messages to members of the charismatic prayer meeting, healings and prophecy. I also provided the same services for Jesus at my job and other activities I attended after the seminar.

I learned from Jesus to do what I was told. I was not to worry about the outcome. It is up to the person to know what to do with the message.

I asked Jesus to teach me more about faith and he did through the example of the story of the grain of salt in my eye and the story about my sinus headache in mass. Both stories taught me how to trust in Jesus.

I was thankful with the spiritual gifts I was given—faith, messages, discernment, wisdom, knowledge, casting out evil, healing, counseling, speaking in tongues, interpretation in tongues and prophecy. Jesus reiterated that the spiritual gifts are irrevocable.

As we move into chapter nine, "…God's people are called to mature both as individuals and as a whole body" (Berardino, 40).

Chapter 9

Week 9: The Church Alive

"Let us not grow tired of doing good, for in due time we shall reap our harvest, if we do not give up. So then, while we have the opportunity, let us do good to all, but especially to those who belong to the family of faith" (Galatians 6:9, 10)

In the ninth week, Jesus told me that He was talking directly to me in prayer instead of the Holy Spirit. When we were given the Novena booklet to help us to connect with the Holy Spirit, I started reading the booklet and realized I was already praying and listening to Jesus. Jesus reminded me of the Trinity, three in one, God, the Son, and the Holy Spirit.

Jesus taught me how to avoid the struggle between earth and the spiritual realm by learning how to ask Him to tell us what to do. He told me I must clear my mind to do God's work. I knew I could not worry and have problems on my mind to do my spiritual assignments. I got up every morning and began my day with prayer and listening to Jesus. Jesus told me to just deliver the message and not to worry about the outcome. He told me that when I delivered the message, some people would be grateful, some would be happy, some ashamed, and some would think they did not need help. It was up to the person receiving the message to understand it and do something with it.

Jesus told me that it was not true that we have to suffer here on earth. It depended on your divine path. He said I was obedient and deserved to live well. He continued saying that God had mighty plans for me. He wanted me to stay focused and to stay the course. He said I now had faith. Ask and it shall be given—thank you, Jesus.

Jesus also reinforced my signature story for faith about the grain of salt/sand in my eye. He also gave me permission to be able to help my family. I prayed to be able to help my family how Jesus had me to help other people. Thank you, Jesus. Again, I was assigned to drive out another demon in a colleague this week. I also counseled and continued to be obedient to Jesus.

One of the last things that Jesus told me in this week was that I would be working with a lot of ministers and clergymen and that they would be the worst to work with. He said that they were battling with Him, Jesus Christ. It was a reflection on their faith in Him. On the other hand, there would be ministers and clergymen who would will be very grateful.

Here are my journal entries for the ninth week of my seminar.

Week 9, Day 1: Saturday, November 21, 2009

"We are called to participate in a unified love wherein we grow into the full likeness of Jesus Christ" (Berardino, 40).

Thank you, Jesus for giving me this wonderful opportunity to grow into the full likeness of you.

Good morning, dear Jesus. Do you have anything to say?

Yes. You are obedient. You do what is expected of you. I am pleased with you. Everyone isn't as obedient as you. We have more work to do.

Yes, Jesus.

Week 9, Day 2: Sunday, November 22, 2009

"Real love is meant to be expressed in concrete action" (Berardino, 40).

"The way we came to know love is that he laid down his life for us; so we ought to lay down our lives for our brothers. If someone who has worldly means sees a brother in need and refuses him compassion, how can the love of God remain in him? Children, let us love not in word or speech but indeed and truth" (1 John 3:16–18).

I understand to love in concrete action. Not from the Father but from the world.

Good morning, dear Jesus. Do you have anything to say?

Yes. Time is here to do more work. Today you will go to church and you will be approached by the priest. He is ready to speak to you now. Take time out today to speak to him. He is hurting inside. He is disappointed in the parish in not supporting the charismatic faith. He wants to talk about what happened over the phone and other experiences you have had. He doesn't really want to talk about him. He wants to talk about you. However, when you talk to him you will discuss his need to truly believe that everything he does I am doing it. It is not him but me.

There are things he wants to do. He needs to ask me what I want him to do. He must understand that he needs to be totally led by me, Jesus, and not to go back and forth. He is frustrated because of what he wants to do. He needs to stop and ask me what should he do. He needs to let go of his earthly side, his worldly side. You may talk about your experiences, but you are to make sure you deliver the message of him needing to get all of his directions from me, not just the parts he wants to do. You will know what to say when you talk to him, for I know you are obedient and will do as I say. The priest is not as obedient as you, and he needs to start being more obedient. Go now. Go in peace. I have spoken.

Thank you Jesus.

Dear Jesus, may I ask you a question? We were given the Novena booklet to read to help us get to hear God's word. You will hear it through hearing the Holy Spirit. I was hearing Jesus Christ not the Holy Spirit.

Yes. You do not need to read this Novena booklet. You already have the gifts. You are already talking to me. Go now. Go in peace.

Thank you, Jesus.

Jesus, may I ask you another question? I wondered if I was listening to the Holy Spirit or was I listening to Him, Jesus Christ.

Yes. The Holy Spirit is the third part of the Trinity, the Father, the Son, and the Holy Spirit. You are not talking to the Holy Spirit. You are talking to me, Jesus Christ. Some do talk to the Holy Spirit. You are the chosen one. You talk directly to me, Jesus Christ. Go now. Go in peace. I have spoken.

Thank you, Jesus.

Week 9, Day 3: Monday, November 23, 2009

"Jesus revealed to us that what we do or fail to do to others is in effect treating him the same way" (Berardino, 41).

> When the son of man comes in his glory, and all the angels with him, he will sit upon his glorious throne, and all the nations will be assembled before him. And he will separate them from one another, as a shepherd separates the sheep from the goats. He will place the sheep on his right and the goats on his left. Then the king will say to those on his right, 'Come, you who are blessed by my Father. Inherit the kingdom prepared for you from the foundation of the world. For I was hungry and you gave me food, I was thirsty and you gave me drink, a stranger and you welcomed me, naked and you clothed me, ill and you cared for me, in prison and you visited me. Then the righteous will answer him and say, 'Lord, when did we see you hungry and feed you, or thirsty and gave you drink? When did we see you a

stranger and welcome you, or naked and clothe you? When did we see you ill or in prison, and visit you? And the king will say to them in reply, Amen, I say to you, whatever you did for one of these least brothers of mine, you did for me.' Then he will say to those on his left, depart from me, you accursed, into the eternal fire prepared for the devil and his angels. For I was hungry and you gave me no food, I was thirsty and you gave me no drink, a stranger and you gave me no welcome, naked and you gave me no clothing, ill and in prison, and you did not care for me. Then they will answer and say, 'Lord, when did we see you hungry or thirsty or a stranger or naked or ill or in prison, and not minister to your needs? He will answer them, 'Amen, I say to you, what you did not do for one of these least ones, you did not do for me.' And these will go off to eternal punishment, but the righteous to eternal life (Matt. 25:31–46).

Good morning, dear Jesus. Do you have anything to say?

Yes. You are obedient. You will do what I tell you. That is why I have chosen you for special assignments. You are working today. Today you will go to school and one of your students is going to approach you. She is extremely upset and needs counsel. You will counsel her. She will feel better afterwards.

The time is near for you to begin casting out evil again. This time it is with someone who knows that something is wrong with her. She doesn't know what to do. She will come to you asking if there is anything you can do. She knows that you cast out the devil in another student because he told her. You will lay your hands on her. You will cast the demon out of her. Immediately, she will feel better and she will thank you. Don't worry about what to say. You will know at the time when it happens.

You are coming along well. In this business of saving souls, some will be grateful, some happy, some ashamed, and some who may think they did not need help. Just obey. Do not worry about outcomes because they will be different. However, they will be far more grateful and happy than you can ever imagine.

Life is going to become very good for you. You are obedient and you deserve to live well. It is not true that you have to suffer here on earth. It depends on your divine path. You will be rewarded on earth and in heaven. God has mighty plans for you. Stay focused. Stay the course. You are doing what I expect of you. I love you and all of God's people. Ask and it shall be given. You now have faith. Your signature story for faith will be the grain of salt in your eye. Yes, a grain of salt was put into your eye to test your faith and you passed. You knew what to say and it worked.

We have talked a long time today. I must clear your mind for the tasks ahead of you. You must be focused as you can see with the priest. He just needed to be reminded to clear his mind of worry so he can do God's work. You must remember to keep your mind clear so you can do God's work. I know you will because you are obedient. Go now. Go in peace. God has spoken.

Thank you, Jesus, for helping me clear my mind to do God's work. I love you and I am ever so humble to listen and follow your word. Through the grace of God I walk in the light of Jesus Christ.

Everything I need to know shall be revealed to me. Everything I need shall be provided for me. Only right and just action is taking place in my life. Thank you, Jesus.

***

I counseled the student at school today. She was a past student from a previous class I taught. I didn't remember everything I said to her, but I told her I knew she was going to come to me today because Jesus told me. I also made sure that she knew that Jesus was answering her prayer and that Jesus was talking to her through me. I was just a channel/vessel for Jesus. She knew. She said I had been on her mind for a week, so when she saw me in the classroom after my class was over, she came over to speak to me.

Dear Jesus, may I ask you a question? Sometimes you tell me things that are going to happen but they might not happen that day.

Yes. Everything is going as planned. You have already spoken with the student who needed counsel. You now need to wait for the student who needs an exorcism to come to you. She will approach you this evening. You are doing a good job. Go now. Go in peace.

The student did not approach me that evening. I know it will happen; it's just a matter of time.

Week 9, Day 4: Tuesday, November 24, 2009

"Sometimes our doing good may seem to be pointless and accomplishing little. But scripture exhorts us not to give up" (Berardino, 42).

"Let us not grow tired of doing good, for in due time we shall reap our harvest, if we do not give up. So then, while we have the opportunity, let us do good to all, but especially to those who belong to the family of faith" (Gal. 6:9, 10).

I will never give up, dear Jesus. I know good always over powers evil.

Good morning, dear Jesus. Do you have anything to say?

Yes. Everything is going as planned. You are doing a good job. The student yesterday did not come to class, but she will come and she is going to ask you if you can help her like you helped the other student. We must move forward with our work in helping souls. Today you will cast out a demon in your colleague. She is going to muster up the courage to ask you today. She is having a hard time sleeping at night and concentrating. She will call you into her office. You will speak tongues to cast out the demon in her. She has had this demon for a very long time. She is going to feel so relieved afterwards that she is going to just keep thanking you. Remember, you are to say, "It is not I, but the Father above. It was Jesus Christ that drove out the demon." Don't worry; you will have enough time before your call to do it. Go now. Go in peace. God has spoken.

Dear Jesus, may I ask you a question? I was wondering if Jesus meant if I would have enough time before my call to do it. Did he mean for me to call in His message this morning?

Yes. It is call. Keep what I say with the words that I give you even though it may not make sense to you.

Thank you Jesus, I will be obedient. I wasn't sure, that's why I asked. Thank you Jesus, I love you.

Week 9, Day 5: Wednesday, November 25, 2009

I needed to treat people that I encountered as my neighbor and I needed to treat them with compassion.

> Jesus replied, "A man fell victim to robbers as he went down to Jerusalem to Jericho. They stripped and beat him and went off leaving him half-dead. A priest happened to be going down that road, but when he saw him, he passed by on the opposite side. Likewise a Levite came to the place, and when he saw him, he passed by on the opposite side. But a Samaritan traveler who came upon him was moved with compassion at the sight. He approached the victim, poured oil and wine over his wounds and bandaged them. Then he lifted him up on his own animal, took him to an inn and cared for him. The next day he took out two silver coins and gave them to the innkeeper with the instruction, "Take care of him. If you spend more than I have given you, I shall repay you on my way back." Which of these three, in your opinion, was neighbor to the robber's victim? He answered, "The one who treated him with mercy. Jesus said to him, Go and do likewise" (Luke 10:30–37).

Good morning, dear Jesus. Do you have anything to say?

Yes. You are going to work today. A student at school is going to approach you about how she is feeling. She knows you drove out a demon in another student. He told her. You are going to lay your hands on her and drive out the demon in her. You will know what to say when the time comes to drive out the demon. She is going to feel relieved immediately. She is going to thank you. Make sure you let her know that, 'It is not I, but the Father above. Jesus Christ drove out the demon.' She is going to be ever so grateful to you.

Word is going to start spreading among the students of your special gifts. Students are going to start coming up to you and asking you to do certain things for them. You must tell them how it works. First, they must pray to me, Jesus, for help. Tell them that you can only do what Jesus tells you to do. They will understand. Sometimes I will tell you right there on the spot to go ahead and do it, but only if I tell you. I know that you will be obedient. That's why I chose you. Go now. Go in peace. I have spoken.

Thank you, Jesus, I will obey. I love you and I am ever so grateful and humbled for you choosing me.

Dear Jesus, may I ask another question?

Yes. She did not come today. You will see her next week. She will ask you next week. The other student is getting stronger and stronger. He is telling other students what you did for him. Even though it may not appear from his behavior, he is very grateful for your obedience in casting out the demon. Go now, go in peace.

Thank you, Jesus.

Week 9, Day 6: Thursday, November 26, 2009

"The Lord calls us to have special respect for the spiritual leaders whose task it is to care for God's flock—the church" (Berardino, 43).

> We ask you brothers, to respect those who are laboring among you and who are over you in the Lord and who admonish you, and show esteem for them with special love on account of their work. Be at peace among yourselves. We urge you brothers, admonish the idle, cheer your fainthearted, support the weak, be patient with all. See that no one returns evil for evil; rather, always seek what is good [both] for each other and for all (1 Thess. 5:12–15).

I have the utmost respect for the pope and the clergy of the Catholic Church.

Good morning, dear Jesus. Do you have anything to say?

Yes. The work has begun. We will work today. I know you wanted the day off to just relax. There is too much work to do to save souls.

I know it is a lot for you to do, but this must be done. You will help your family today because they are in dire need for healing. They are faithful to God and deserve their prayers being answered. You will not approach any of them. They will come to you. If they do not come to you then they are not ready. They must be receptive and ready for me to heal them and they will be. Your family is going to be the first to recognize your spiritual gifts. You will be the talk among your relatives today. They are going to want to sit and hear some of your experiences. Yes, the time has begun for your spiritual journey ministering publicly among the people, because for years you have already started ministering among the people. You were so obedient when you discovered that you were a minister among the people. Don't worry about remembering everything to do. When the time comes when they walk up to you, you will remember what to do and say. The words will come just like they came before when you were doing God's work.

You are healing your family. You prayed for it and you will be able to help your family just like you are going to help millions and billions of others. You are going to be known worldwide. I know this is hard for you to give up your personal life, but you will have your husband and family around you. They will never forget this Thanksgiving Day. Go now. Go in peace. I have spoken.

Dear Jesus, may I ask you a question? I did not meet a husband during the nine-week seminar, but I have met someone special in my life a few years ago. I was thinking if I could share this message with my prayer partner.

Yes. You can tell your prayer partner. She already knows that it is going to be a special day today. She is going to be quietly praying all day today.

Thank you, Jesus.

***

Good evening, Jesus. May I ask you a question? I wondered what was going on. My family did not approach me during Thanksgiving. Nothing happen today the way Jesus said it would.

Yes. Today was not a good day. Your family is not ready to heal.

Week 9, Day 7: Friday morning, November 27, 2009

I know, Jesus, that all I do for you during my earthly journey will have a heavenly reward. In fact it is in heaven where my most valuable and true possessions will be.

"Do not store up for yourselves treasures on earth, where moth and decay destroy, and thieves break in and steal. But store up treasures in heaven, where neither moth nor decay destroys, nor thieves break in and steal. For where your treasure is, there also will your heart be" (Matt. 6: 19–21).

Good morning, dear Jesus. Do you have anything to say?

Yes. It was quite a day yesterday. People are not ready to accept their blessing. They pray for it and yet in their hearts they do not believe that it will happen even when it does. It is so important to have faith. Faith is not easy. People talk about it, but they don't really understand how to use faith. You have to believe. Your family is not ready to believe. But don't worry. In time they will.

You are doing a good job. Don't be discouraged. Remember some will be happy, some will not know, some will ask, and some will not. In the long run they all will eventually get to the truth and know. Most of them will know; the others will be in denial for one reason or another.

You have come a long way. You do believe and obey. That is why I chose you. You truly understand. You are so knowledgeable that they cannot comprehend where you are. People know you have special gifts even when they don't know exactly what they are.

Stay on course. Continue your divine path. You are doing a great job obeying. Just focus on obeying. You cannot control other people's outcomes. They do that. As you become more and more known, people will begin to believe more and will have better outcomes. Just remember outcomes are on them, not you. You are a vessel. It is I, Jesus Christ, who they do not truly believe in. Remember the church member? She said she knew I was trying to convince her. At least she was honest with herself and knew she had to pray for me to give her the faith to truly believe. You will encounter people like your church member from time to time. They may not say that to you, but they will know.

You will work a lot with the ministry and clergymen. They will be the most difficult to work with. They think they already have the calling and don't really need any person to help them. Don't worry. The ministry and clergymen are battling with me, Jesus Christ, not you. It is hard for some to believe a layperson would have such holiness compared to ministers and clergymen who have committed their lives to me. On the other hand, there will be many ministers and clergymen who will be ever so grateful. Remember, it is a reflection on their faith in me, Jesus.

Don't get discouraged. We have a lot of work ahead of us. You are not to worry about anything. All of your needs will be met. Go now. Go in peace. I have spoken.

Thank you, dear Jesus.

Dear Jesus, may I ask you a question? My niece is on the spiritual level with you. She wondered if her mother knows.

Yes. Don't worry about her. She will be all right. She asked you if her mother knows, because she doesn't want her mother to know. She was relieved when you said no. She does not know you yet. You are not into this earthly world for recognition. You are truly about your spirituality. That's why I chose you. You are truly spiritually based.

Thank you, Jesus.

***

I was reflecting back on the Thanksgiving holiday time. My oldest daughter did not attend the family Thanksgiving dinner. My sister made a plate for her to give to her on Friday. We went to the movies Friday. During the movies with my oldest daughter, I started looking over my glasses and noticed I could see clearer without them. I thanked Jesus for letting me see without my glasses. I finished watching the movie, *2010*, without them. I drove home to get the Thanksgiving dinner my sister made for my oldest daughter the night before. I then drove her home without wearing my glasses. I kept thanking Jesus all the way home.

Dear Jesus, may I ask a question?

Yes. Your vision will progressively get better and better depending on your faith. You were able to drive tonight without your glasses. This was a big step because you have night blindness where you cannot read signs, but you were able to read them tonight. In time you will not have to wear glasses at all. Go now. Go in peace. I have spoken.

Thank you, Jesus.

Saturday, November 28, 2009

After completing the seminar, I was well on my way to praying through listening to Jesus every morning.

Good morning, Jesus. Do you have anything to say?

Yes. There is still work to do. You will have to go to church this morning. The priest wants to talk to you. He knows that you are strong in the Word. He will approach you. You will counsel him. He is still a little depressed. You will talk to him and he will feel better afterwards. Do not worry about what to say. You will know what to say when you talk to him. Remember, I am talking to him through you. Go now. Go in peace.

I went to church this morning and the priest was not there. I waited in the car for a few minutes before asking Jesus if I could leave.

Dear Jesus, may I ask you a question?

Yes. Everything is going as planned. You are doing what you are told to do. Don't worry; you will get a chance to talk to the priest. It is just a matter of time. You are going to do some shopping today. You will come across a woman who is very depressed and will just begin talking to you about her troubles. You will know who it is as soon as she approaches you. You will take the time to listen to her. You will counsel her, and she will feel better afterwards. You will then be approached by a man who is old and weary. He is just waiting to cross the other side. He will also tell you his problems. You will counsel again. People who see you know there is something different about you.

They know that they can talk to you and you will help them to feel better. You will counsel and get the things you need to get. Go now. Go in peace. I have spoken.

Thank you Jesus

***

In week nine, Jesus said it is not true that you have to suffer on earth. It depends on your divine path. He said avoid the struggle between earth and the spiritual realm by learning how to ask Jesus to tell us what to do. I don't worry anymore and if by chance I do, I ask Jesus to guide me. When delivering messages to people, I am directed by Jesus to give them. Jesus reminded me to just deliver the message and do not worry about the outcome. It is up to the person receiving the message to understand the message and to do something with it. The person will know if it is their message or not.

When the time came to learn how to listen to the Holy Spirit, the participants were given a Novena Booklet to read to help them to become closer to the Holy Spirit. As I began to read it, Jesus told me I was already listening to Him (Jesus Christ). Jesus also told me how my faith has been strengthening through my experiences with him. I had testimonies of my faith through my experiences with the grain of salt in my eye and the sinus headache I had during mass in church.

One of the last things Jesus said to me was that I would be working with a lot of ministers and clergymen and they may be the worst to work with. It happens because they are battling with their faith, with Him (Jesus). On the other hand, there will be ministers and clergymen that will be very grateful.

I thank Jesus for allowing me to have a very close relationship with Him. May God be the glory.

Chapter 10

Conclusion

"To one is given through the spirit the expression of wisdom; to another the expression of knowledge according to the same spirit; to another faith by the same spirit; to another gifts of healing by the one spirit; to another mighty deeds; to another prophecy; to another discernment of spirits; to another a variety of tongues; to another interpretation of tongues" (1 Corinthians 12:8–10)

This was a book about spirituality. It was about my relationship with Jesus Christ. For most, it will be about the Holy Spirit. I have had the honor of being able to speak with Jesus directly. In my quest and thirst to have a special relationship with Jesus, I took a seminar at my parish. I am baptized in the Spirit through my special relationship with Jesus. Each day of the seminar brought me closer and closer to Jesus. Jesus will use you as much as you allow Him to through our obedience to Him.

At first, I did not have a pattern or rhythm in praying and communicating with Jesus on a daily basis. As each week went by, I would begin my day reading the scriptures and daily readings. I would wait and listen for Jesus to speak to me. I began to realize that I could have a conversation with Him. I could ask Him questions and He would answer me. Wow! I would have the most unreal sensation flowing through my body. I felt like I was floating in the air. Jesus is so good to us. He is kind and loving. He is always forgiving.

I have received many gifts from Jesus. Regardless of how many you receive, be obedient to the Holy Spirit. Do as the Holy Spirit tells you. Once you have received your gift(s) they are irrevocable. You must walk the walk, as they say, and be obedient. It will not always be easy. At times, it may also take courage.

Many of you will be able to relate to this book in some way, shape, or form. If you did not, you will in the near future. There is no coincidence that you read this book. It was in your destiny. It is in your quest to learn more about God the Father, the Son, and the Holy Spirit. It is time for you to connect and either become closer to God or actually begin your journey with the Holy Spirit. If you are not baptized by the Spirit, you will be soon. Being baptized by the Spirit is having a special relationship with Him.

By reading this book of my journey of becoming closer to Jesus, it will bring you closer to Him, too. Your thirst to want a relationship with the Holy Spirit has brought you this far. To quench your thirst, take a few minutes to just relax and breathe deeply. Ask the Holy Spirit to come into your heart and teach you how the two of you may have an intimate relationship. Ask the Holy Spirit to speak to you.

Be still and listen as if someone is trying to whisper in your ear. Now be quiet. Be still and write down in a journal what words He has to give you for today. Do not try to understand what is being said until the Holy Spirit has finished speaking to you. You will then read what you wrote for comprehension. This will be a very special day for you.

For those of you who already know how to listen to the Holy Spirit, you will also take a few minutes to listen and write down what the Holy Spirit has to say to you. It will be something very special just for you.

It has been a long time getting to this point in my life. Things happened a little at a time. Jesus will use you as much as you allow by being obedient to His Word. Sometimes you will be afraid to do what He tells you because sometimes God tests you to see how obedient you will be. Many times people pray for Jesus to give them gifts they cannot or do not have the courage to use. They often look at the glamour side of the gift. Many of you will experience similar activities that you read in this book, or you will begin to feel some of the experiences shortly.

There are no mistakes in the universe. You were meant to read this book. You will receive a blessing from this book as you finish reading it. Always remember: "Jesus loves you, Jesus will take care of you, Jesus will provide for you, Jesus will protect you, and Jesus is here for you 24/7" (from Dr. Jacki's Morning Prayer). I told my spiritual story. *My Spiritual Awakening. Look What Happened to Me. Is it Happening to You Too?"*

Jacqueline Parker Scott, EdD, MBA

References/Spiritual Scriptures

Week 1: Jesus is Lord
John 6:35, 37
2 Corinthians 8:9
Philippians 2:5–11
Romans 5: 6–8
John 14:6
Hebrews 2:9–11
Colossians 1:15–20
Matthews 6:9-13
Thessalonians 5:17
Psalm 66:1–4
Philippians 4:6–7
Ephesians 1:5–6
Ephesians 6:18
1 Corinthians 14:2, 15

Week 2: God Our Father
Matthew 11:27
Ephesians 4:5, 6
Romans 8:15–17
John 15:16
Matthew 18:14–16
Colossians 3:17
Psalms 62:6–9

Week 3: Wholesomeness in Love
Matthew 6:12
1 Peter 2:24
Luke 5:31, 32
Romans 8:1, 2
James 5:16
John 8:31, 32
Psalms 51:1–4

Week 4: The Helper
Mark 1:8
John 16:13, 14
Ephesians 5:18–19
Romans 5:5
1 Corinthians 2:10–12
Jude 20
John 7:37–39

Week 5: Following Jesus
Acts 4:29–30
Psalms 32:8
Ephesians 5:18–19
Romans 5:5
1 Corinthians 2:10–-12
St Jude 20

Week 6: The Fruit of the Spirit
Galatians 5:22
Matthews 8:13
Matthew 9:28–29
Galatian 5:16–23
1 Corinthians 13:13
Philippians 4:6, 7
2 Peter 1:3–8

Week 7: Spiritual Warfare	Week 8: The Gifts of the Spirit
Ephesians 6:10–11	1 Corinthians 12:4
Genesis 17:5	Luke 12:48
Genesis 17:15	Matthew 17:20–21
Genesis 35:10	Hebrews 2:1–4
Colossians 1:11–14	James 1:17
Hebrews 2:14–15	Isaiah 11:2
Matthew 9:27–30	1 Corinthians 2:11–14
Matthew 21:22	
James 4:7	
Ephesians 6:10–18	
Romans 16:19, 20	
Ephesians 2:1–5	
Acts 26:16–18	

Week 9: The Church Alive

Week 10: Conclusion

Galatians 6:9, 10

1 Corinthians 12:8–12

1 John 3:16–18

Matthew 25:31–46

Galatians 6:9, 10

Luke 10:30–37

Thessalonians 5:12–15

Matthew 6:19–21

Berardino, D. *Thy Kingdom Come.* SCRC: Burbank, CA, 1997.

www.ingramcontent.com/pod-product-compliance
Lightning Source LLC
LaVergne TN
LVHW041620070426
835507LV00008B/356